# Barcelona lo tiene todo

Vincenzo Berghella

Copyright Page

Copyright year: 2017

ISBN No: 978-0-578-20084-2

From the same author:

- **Obstetric Evidence Based Guidelines.** Informa Healthcare, London, UK, and New York, USA (2007) [English]

- **Maternal Fetal Evidence Based Guidelines.** Informa Healthcare, London, UK, and New York, USA (2007) [English]

- **Laughter, the best medicine. Jokes for everyone.** (2007) [English]

- **Ridere, la migliore medicina. Barzellette per bambini.** (2007) [Italiano]

- **My favorite quotes.** (2009) [English]

- **In medio stat virtus – Citazioni d'autore.** (2009) [Italiano]

- **Quello che di voi vive in me.** (2009) [Italiano]

- **Dall'altra parte dell'oceano.** (2010) [Italiano] (Translated in: **On the other side of the ocean.** (2013) [English])

- **Preterm Birth: Prevention and Management.** Wiley-Blackwell. Oxford, United Kingdom. (2010) [English]

- **From father to son.** (2010) [English]

- **Sollazzi.** (2010) [Italiano]

- **The land of religions.** (2011) [English] (Translated in: **La terra delle religioni.** (2013) [Italiano])

- **Giramondo.** (2011) [Italiano]

- **Obstetric Evidence Based Guidelines.** Informa Healthcare, London, UK, and New York, USA (2012; Second Edition) [English]

- **Maternal Fetal Evidence Based Guidelines.** Informa Healthcare, London, UK, and New York, USA (2012; Second Edition) [English]

- **Trip to London.** (2012) [English]

- **Il primo amore non si scorda mai.** (2012) [Italiano]

- **Maldives.** (2013) [English]

- **Russia.** (2013) [English]

- **Happiness: the scientific path to achieving wellbeing.** (2014) [English] (Translated in **Felicita': il percorso scientifico per raggiungere il benessere** [Italian])

- **New Zealand: 100% pure.** (2014) [English]

- **Me dentro: i primi scritti dai 17 ai 20 anni** (2015) [Italiano]

- **Me dentro: alla ricerca dell'amore** (2015) [Italiano]

- **US Rowing Youth Nationals** (2015) [English]

- **Polynesia** (2016) [English]

- **Obstetrics: Normal and Problem Pregnancies** (Gabbe, Niebyl, Simpson, Landon, Galan, Janiaus, Driscoll, Berghella, Grobman). Elsevier, Philadelphia, USA (2016; Seventh Edition) [English]

- **Obstetric Evidence Based Guidelines.** CRC Press, London, UK, and New York, USA (2017; Third Edition) [English]

- **Maternal Fetal Evidence Based Guidelines.** CRC Press, London, UK, and New York, USA (2017; Third Edition) [English]

- **Operative Obstetrics.** (Apuzzio, Vintzileos, Berghella, Alvarez-Perez) CRC Press, London, UK, and New York, USA (2017; Fourth Edition) [English]

- **Krakow and Auschwitz.** (2017) [English]

- **Chennai and Coimbatore, India.** (2018) [English]

- **M'zav, Algeria.** (2018) [English]

- **Labor and Delivery: Evidence Based Management.** (Berghella, Saccone, Ghi, Roman) JayPee Brothers, India (2018) [English]

Barcelona Neighborhood Overview

From Rick Steves' Guide

## Before the flight

There are some goals you achieve when young, and others that take some more time to get to. I have always liked to travel, and have done a fair amount of it. As an Italian by birth, you would have thought I would have gotten to nearby Spain a long time ago. But I'm 53 when the opportunity comes and I can finally grab it.

Spain has always been in my plans. It's a country that I have always felt close to my heart. I have always been fascinated by its glorious as well as at times complex history. I love its multicultural and multireligious history. Italy is full of Spanish influences, especially the south, where my mother is from. America was discovered by an Italian on Spanish ships, and he certainly changed my life, as it's now been 33 plus years that I've lived in the USA.

I have close Spanish friends such as Tedi (short for Teresa). High school friends such as Paolo, former mentees such as Ilaria, and wonderful collaborators such as Montse, all live in Spain. Paola has been to Spain, and she has always described it as a wonderful place to visit.

So when Moshe Hod, my Israeli colleague who organizes many wonderful conferences in our field of maternal-fetal medicine – high-risk pregnancy – invited me to the DIP2017 meeting here in Barcelona from March 8-11 2017, I could not refuse.

DIP stands for Diabetes in Pregnancy, which is Moshe's main interest, but this 9th DIP meeting (I've already been to a couple of them in the years past) is a huge meeting with a lot more topics covered. There will be over 1200 attendees from dozens of different countries.

I prepare the trip by reading a bit the two guides that our son Andrea has bought for his trip to Spain in the summer of 2016. I'm particularly fascinated by the history of Spain. I begin to highlight the major sites to visit, the 'musts,' which are also in my adored '1,000 places to see before you die.'

In one of the several emails I get from the organizers before the conference, Moshe states that on Wednesday March 8, just as the congress is starting, Barcelona will be playing against Paris Saint Germain (PSG) for the return leg of the quarter final of the European Champions league.

As soon as I learn of this option, I tell Moshe I absolutely would like to get a ticket. Other European speakers, copied in the email, also show interest. Moshe promises to try to get tickets for all of us through the organization. But a couple of weeks go by with no news. I keep up the pressure with more emails.

Eventually, one of the staffers confirms that I will have a ticket to the game waiting for me at the congress reception! I've never been at the Camp Nou, Barcelona famous soccer pitch, which holds over 90,000 spectators. I cannot wait!

If I have one major vice, it's watching soccer. It's in my blood. The first leg of this confrontation, played in Paris, had an incredible result: PSG, the underdog, defeated Barcelona 4 to 0. I think the return leg could be somewhat boring, with PSG defending, and probably Barcelona unable to score more than 4 goals on them, especially without conceding any.

**Tuesday March 7, 2017**

I Uber it from work to the Philadelphia airport, as usual now. I can leave at 4:30pm, later than I usually do for when I'm going to Italy, as the flight, originally scheduled to take off at 6:40pm, has been delayed until 8pm. Airlines still recommend to get to the airport in plenty of time, and so I do. By 5pm I've passed passport control, and baggage control, which today have very short lines.

American Airlines and British Airlines are part of the same frequent flyer plan (One World), so while I'm flying BA today I hope I can still enjoy the AA VIP lounge. In fact, the nice receptionists let me in, and I can relax. I have two different soups, some carrots and a hummus spread, as well as some cookies, of course.

I also make some phone calls. I talk with my good friend Don. I do a video WhatsApp call with Paola and Pietro. Pietro is a junior in high school, an 11th grader, and is deciding which colleges to visit, and to eventually apply. He is also evaluating if and when to retake the SAT, or to take the ACT.

My plane as I said was supposed to leave at 6:40pm from Philadelphia International Airport, and get in Heathrow in London, UK, at 6:40a. There I should switch terminals, from 5 where I'm supposed to land, to 3 where I'll have to catch the London-Barcelona flight, leaving at 9:55am and arriving in Barcelona at around 1pm.

So I'm a bit worried that with the delay I'll miss the connection. I go back to the AA VIP lounge receptionist and make sure they'll announce when the BA flight will leave. She assures me again, as she had done when I first walked in, that they will. At around 7pm though, done will all my eating, calls, and work on the computer, I decide to head for the gate anyway.

I walk leisurely towards Gate 16. As I get closer, I see only a few people sitting around the gate; in fact, I notice a short line of passengers going through the gate. I look at the diplay information, and notice the new departing time is 7:30pm! The last 20 or so passengers are boarding, everyone else is on the plane already! I would have missed the plane had I stayed a bit more in the lounge. They never announced the new departing time, and when boarding started. I'm a bit stressed, but glad I am nonetheless making it on the plane.

On board, I review again what to do in Barcelona. I look at my busy schedule of talks at the DIP conference, and the parts where I can sneak out and do some Barcelona sightseeing. Later I get a headache, which I try to treat by sleeping. My rest is helpful but not curative, so eventually I take three ibuprofens and later I'm able to sleep.

When I fly and feel turbulence, I think of what a great life I've had, and that I'm not afraid of dying anymore. I am not afraid of flying anymore either. At all. I enjoy it. I have a great time writing, or reading, or watching movies, or talking to the person next to me. I've had an incredible life, and while I want to get a lot more done, I would die a happy, accomplished man today.

As we arrive over London, the city is covered by clouds, like usual.

## Wednesday March 8th, 2017

It's amazing how big Heathrow is. I walk for miles to get from Terminal 5, where we land, to Terminal 3; and I also have to take two trains to get there. But I do make it on time, and take off with my London-Barcelona British Airways flight. I sleep some more on this shorter flight.

As we head south, the clouds dissipate, and the view gets more and more amazing. I see the Pyrenees, with some peaks covered in snow. I also continue to read a bit about my destination.

Over Spain, there are no clouds at all, just sun sun sun! We land a bit late but not bad, around 1:45pm. From 16:30 (4:30pm) until 17:30 (5:30pm) I'm supposed to moderate the second session of the congress. This DIP congress starts today at 15:00 (3pm). I should be able to make it.

My carry-on, which had been checked in London, comes out quickly at the efficient baggage claim. I'm so happy to be in Spain. I call Paola, and then my parents, to reassure them all I arrived safely, to try to transmit to them some of my enthusiasm, and to check that all is good with them, too.

As usual, I chat away with the taxi driver, who does not speak a word of English. He accepts my Italian/Spanish mix as if I'm fluent in his language. I get into the hotel by 2:30pm. And what a hotel! The Fairmont Juan Carlos I (named after the father of the current king of Spain, much beloved in this country) is huge, modern, luxurious, mostly glass and steel.

Probably disheveled from the long travel but excited, I approach the check-in desk. To my surprise and delight, in the terrace on the first floor overlooking this main huge entrance hall, I see Verratti and Pastore chatting! These are two of the best players from PSG.

Indeed Moshe had said the PSG players would be staying at our hotel, which is very close to the pitch, the Camp Nou. And the taxi driver had confirmed it to me. But to see one of my heroes right away on my walking in is more than I could have dreamed for.

Marco Verratti is a 24 year old star who was born and raised in my region, Abruzzo, in Italy. In fact, his small town, Manoppello, is less than 10 kilometers from my original city, Pescara. Our sons Andrea and Pietro and I even saw him strolling in Pescara about 3 years ago, when he was less well known. We shamelessly stopped him, and asked to take a couple of pictures with him. He was supernice, and friendly. In my lifetime never a soccer player from my parts had become so famous so quickly, now even a starting midfielder and leading player in our Italian national team. Forza Verratti! I wish Andrea and Pietro were also here with me now.

While in queue at the check-in counter, a thin muscular black guy lines up behind me. I notice he is wearing PSG official gear, and he looks like a footballer. A bit ashamed at my ignorance, I ask, "What's your name?" He says with a smile, "Camara." He is also on the PSG squad! I've heard of him, I should have known. I study too much medicine, darn. So I ask someone nearby to take a picture of me with Camara there in front of the check in. What a nice guy. I thought he would be taller, but I always forget how tall I am.

In my hotel room, on the 7th floor, I shower, change, and look and feel like a new man. I walk out in the sun, and less than 100 yards from the hotel entrance I walk into Palau de Congressos de Catalunya of Barcelona, a beautiful facility. I quickly register and get my badge for admission to the conference halls.

In Hall A, the congress is just starting. I sit down next to my young Italian colleagues, Daniele Di Mascio and Claudia Caissutti. They are two of the 33 residents and young doctors who have spent time training and doing research with me in high-risk pregnancy at Thomas Jefferson University in Philadelphia. They tell me it's been announced that Roberto Romero, one of the main attractions of the conference, did not make it.

So now the opening ceremony is a series of presentations by the organizers of the Congress, as well as other authorities such as the FIGO President and others. There are people from all over the world alternating at the podium.

Before the next session, where I'm directly involved as moderator, I remember one of the most important things! I go back to the Registration Desk and get the tickets for the Barca-PSG game.

My session starts at 4:30pm in the same main hall, still packed with attendees. The three lectures are on complex genetic aspects of pregnancy and pregnancy complications, and are presented by professors from Cyprus, Italy, and Israel. Unfortunately there is no time for questions. We (me and the FIGO president, CN Purandare) as moderators have to also make sure that the session stays on time, and we do not go over 5:40pm, when the next session starts. We manage to do that, as the speakers stay mostly within their allotted time.

After listening to Eduard Gratacos' (the Chair of Ob-Gyn in Barcelona, an excellent researcher) talk, at around 6:30pm, I go back to the hotel to change and get ready for the game. While it's now still warm out, good enough to be just with a shirt, I bring a sweater and a light coat. They'll come in handy.

At about 7pm, the bus for the Camp Nou is supposed to be leaving. I find it at the hotel entrance. I'm not going to miss it! I look and look for some of my colleagues who had expressed interest by email about attending the game, but I do not see any other than Yariv Yogev, a friendly, always smiling chairman of ob-gyn from Israel.

The bus only takes off after 7:30pm, and by then I realize I'm the only one from the DIP congress going to the game who does not speak Hebrew. But they are all nice, and often speak English so I can understand. Despite some traffic, we get to within 50 yards of the Camp Nou within 15 minutes.

Thousands of fans are squirming around, many with huge flags, or decked in Barca gear. I do spot a few quieter PSG fan.

Given the 4-0 result of the first leg, both sets of fans might be a bit less enthusiastic this will be a meaningful game. Darkness, now set in, enhances the many bright lights of the imposing Camp Nou.

With some of my new Israeli friends, we discover the closest entrance, and then find a nice restaurant/bar, where I get a long baguette sandwich for 8 euros. Not too bad given its size, and the game I'm at. Then, zigzagging among tens of thousands of people, we eventually find our seats.

Great seats!! I'm in the first ring, in the front row (!), just over the railing, very close to centerfield! Wow! These tickets were not cheap (Euro 350, don't tell Paola), but they could hardly be better! At the entrance, each of us 90,000 plus attending were given a large Barcelona flag, with the trademark blu-grana (bleu and darkish red) colors. Thousands are already waiving them in the air, and so I join them. What a spectacle.

I also devour my large delicious (I'm hungry I guess) sandwich. I wish my family, my friends, were here. But sometimes you have to go at it alone, and here I had no choice. I'm so happy! Soon the players come out and start warming up on the pick.

On the right side from me, I see Marco Verratti, Javier Pastore - great Argentinian midfielder, Edinson Cavani - the Uruguayan striker who looks like a rebel native Indian, Thiago Motta - the Brazilian midfielder who used to play for my beloved Inter Milan, Thiago Silva - the Brazilian who is one of the best defenders in the world; and I could go on forever about the other PSG players.

On my left, just in fact below me, the Barca players. I should have called them mythological figures actually, as they are SO famous. The best player in the whole world, Leo Messi. Neymar, the Brazilian fabulous winger. Suarez, the Uruguayan striker, known for his viciousness as much as his soccer skills. Gerard Pique', the tall defender and captain.

I know the names and stories of each of the 22 players on the pitch. What an amazing game I'm going to watch. I do not care who wins. I do not care who gets to the next stage. I just want to see them playing well. I do not even know who to root for, which is a bit unusual for me.

Barca is a favorite of mine, since their soccer is so ebullient, unique, elegant, inventive. But Verratti, my hometown hero, plays for PSG. And PSG was the underdog despite their talent against mighty Barcelona, who has won the Champions League already 5 times, most of them in the last 10 years or so.

The team rosters are announced. All the star players are here and fit to play. After the announcement of each of the Barca players, the 90,000 let a loud roar rock the stadium. The Barca official anthem is sang in chorus by the whole stadium. I guess the whole stadium minus a thousand or so PSG fans, tucked way up in one of the curved sections high on the stands. They are loud anyway, even if a small minority and definitively geographically marginalized.

The stage is set. The pitch is impeccable. The weather perfect, clear, upper 60's, the faintest of breezes just enough to wave the flags well. The stars aligned above and below us. With a seating capacity of 99,354, Camp Nou (New Field in Catalan) is the largest stadium in Spain, also the largest in Europe and the third largest association football stadium in the world in terms of capacity. It has hosted two European Cup/Champions League finals in 1989 and 1999, five matches including the opening game of the 1982 FIFA World Cup and the football competition final at the 1992 Summer Olympics.

The first kick, by the Barcelona players, starts the game. I still can't believe I'm here. The task for the Barcelona players is huge. Obviously an early goal would increase their chances, and certainly boost their hopes. Barcelona is quickly on the front foot, attaching. Their football is unique. They never seem to panic. PSG is soon camped in their own half.

Crosses start pouring in the PSG 18yard box. On one of them, by Rafinha, the ball gets a bit loose in the PSG penalty area. The PSG keeper, Trapp, comes out of the goal area to grab the ball, but Suarez is much quicker, and gets to the ball first with his head, pushing it towards the goal line.

A PSG defender seems to have prevented the goal though by heading the ball, very close to the goal line. Suarez and the rest of the Barca players put their hands up and scream for the goal. After a long couple of seconds, the referee blows his whistle and points to midfield. Barca scored!!

Not even 3 minutes have elapsed from the start of the game. Barca still needs 3 more goals just to tie the match, since they lost 4-0 in Paris in the first leg. But now their confidence is a bit higher; Suarez grabs the ball and brings it quickly to midfield, trying to save time. The stadium gets even more excited, fans keep cheering their beloved Barca.

While the Catalans keep on attaching, the game is stuck on 1-0 for most of the first half. Around the 40$^{th}$ minute though, Iniesta, one of Barca's fabled stars - who scored the winning goal for Spain when they won their recent World Cup, gets in the PSG area. The PSG defenders have trouble clearing the ball, so Iniesta heels back a loose ball, which Layvin Kurzawa, one of the PSG defenders, tries to kick out. But he terribly miskicks it, the strange bounce lets the ball arch over the goalie, and it ends up by some strange miracle in the net. Barca 2, PSG 0!

These two goals have probably not been the prettiest, and an own-goal always feels a bit like a theft, but I'm stunned how Barca was somehow able to score again. The first half quickly draws to a close. Barca has made up half of its deficit in half of the time. One would thing PSG will be defending even more in the second half, but certainly Barca's task is easier than when they started.

Cavani starts the second half with the first kick for PSG. Barca is soon attaching again. I'm a bit surprised PSG, which is an awesome team, is playing so defensively. Neymar is playing really well on the left side of Barca's attack. The PSG right back, Thomas Meunier, a player who is excellent at attacking, is having a bit of trouble defending against Neymar. In fact, Verratti, my idol, often doubles up in defending on Neymar.

But on one of his runs, right below where I'm sitting, Neymar goes by Meunier, who falls down alongside Neymar inside the box. Neymar's legs hit Meunier's arms and head, and he falls flat in the box. The whistle's blows quickly: penalty! We are only 5 minutes inside the second half. Wow. I can hardly believe it.

The best player in the world, Lionel Messi, steps to take the penalty kick. The ritual ensues. With his hands on his hips, he looks at the goalie. Then he stares at the ball for what seems like a long time. The referee blows the whistle again, while the stadium is in complete silence. Almost 100,000 people are looking at the ball.

Lionel Messi kicks with his priceless left foot. The ball comes out flying towards Messi's left, the goalie's right. Trapp guesses right, but the ball flies past him, very close but inside the post, about two feet above ground. Perfect penalty, as expected. Messi runs to pick up the ball from the net, and carries it jubilant to midfield again.

The stadium is now roaring. All are on their feet. Barca 3, PSG 0. Only one more goal, and Barca will have made up the biggest deficit ever in a Champions League game. I begin to think this is inevitable. There are at least 40 minutes left to play, Barca will for sure be able to score again. I feel bad for PSG. But elated at the amazing game I'm watching, and happy for the 99,000 plus around me.

Barca keeps on attacking, now really optimistic that fate is on their side. But they get a bit more vulnerable to PSG counterattacks. On one of them, Meunier goes by Neymar, enters the Barca penalty box on Barca's left side, and serves a delightful fast ball to the arriving Cavani. Cavani hits it on a slide, and... hits the post on ter Stegen's (Barca's goalie) left side. Wow! That looked menacing. The stadium gulps. Barca dodged a big bullet.

In Champion league play, if goals are even among the two legs, away goals count double. If PSG scores here at Barcelona, the score would be 3-1. Barca, even with a 5-1 victory, would be even on goals (5-1 and 0-4 would give 5-5), but given that PSG would have scored an away goal, PSG would win the contest and get to the semifinals. So, if PSG scored, Barca would have to score 3 more, and get to 6-1, to qualify for the semis. I think that Barca better watch out.

Around the $62^{nd}$ minute, or $17^{th}$ of the second half, PSG gets a free kick around midfield. Verratti steps up to the ball. He kicks it long, inside Barca's box. In general I do not like soccer being played with long balls. I like fine short passes, elegant plays. But the ball gets perfectly to Kurzawa's head, the PSG defender who had caused the own-goal in the first half. He redirects it towards the penalty spot area.

I look attentively, and I see a fast running Cavani approaching. Amazingly, this gifted striker, who has scored more than a goal per game in the last 36 games, is seemingly uncovered by any Barca defender. How could this be? With a vengeance, he gets to the ball, and strikes it hard with his preferred right foot. The ball flies into the back of Barca's net.

3-1! Wow. I can't believe Barca allowed Cavani to score. Barca was doing so well. Now they have an almost unsurmountable task. They need to score 3 more goals. And there are less than 30 minutes left in the game. No way that's going to happen. They are playing the French champions after all.

The whole stadium quiets down. The elation of a few minutes ago has evaporated. Around me long faces, and very little noise. Silence envelops the air, for the first time one can almost hear exactly what the 11 PSG players are saying to each other on the field; they seem the only ones talking now. Everyone else may have their mouths open, but they are because of silent despair and disbelief.

I continue watching the game, which seems a lot less exciting now. And I also keep on glancing at the big screen, where the game time keeps on ticking. We soon get to the $20^{th}$ minute of the second half. Then to the $30^{th}$ minute. Still 3-1. Still 3 goals for Barca to score in now only 15 minutes plus extra time left.

As we pass the 40$^{th}$ minute of the second half, of the 85$^{th}$ minute of the whole game, with only 5 minutes to go, I do not think there is one person in the stadium with any hope left for Barca to win. The PSG supporters have been singing incessantly since Cavani scored for them.

A few Barca fans start leaving their seats and exiting the stadium. I guess with over 90,000 people leaving this place, some will hit heavy traffic. And this is a weekday, and already kind of late. At least five or six Barca fans just on my right leave as well. They were so excited minutes ago, now they feel defeated, sad, their flags swinging down from their hands to the floor, not being waved madly as when Barca scored the earlier 3 goals.

I ponder if to leave as well. After all, I'm jet lagged, so it's like past 4 in the morning for me, I've had a huge day, with plenty of events, and watched now >90% of the game. But I decide to stay. If I want I can walk back to the hotel, only about a mile – one and a half kilometers – from the stadium.

I want to enjoy this mega event until the end. It's still a beautiful night, I'm at Camp Nou, and I want to watch every last kick, I want to watch the players being applauded at the end, and the fans leave this glorious soccer cathedral.

With less purpose, Barca is still trying to attack. Neymar keeps on being hard to stop. On one of his dribbles, right in front of my seat, he goes past DeMaria, who fouls him just outside the left upper corner of PSG penalty box, looking from Barca's attack. He quickly gets the ball, and is ready to shot.

PSG takes its time organizing the wall. As Neymar kicks the ball, they all jump. Fans are chanting and beating drums in the stands. The ball magically goes over the heads of the players in the wall, and arches smoothly to the goal's left upper corner from where I'm watching. Ter Stegen flies in that direction, but the ball is unstoppable.

The stadium explodes again in a huge happy roar. The Barca players get the ball from the bottom of the net, and sprint back to midfield. It's 4-1 now. I look at the big screen. It's the 88$^{th}$ minute, only 2 minutes left in regulation time. No way Barca can score the needed two extra goals.

I do not think even the Barca fans think their team can score more in so little time. But... This is a game, fun to watch, they paid an expensive ticket... why not cheer their beloved team on??!! I think this is getting pretty interesting now. I just love this game!

The match now is thrilling, especially since the fans are really loud. Barca is certainly more optimistic, you can tell by their more positive playing. But the 90$^{th}$ minute goes by. The referee decides for 5 extra minutes of play. I'm less optimistic than the Barca fans, but happy to enjoy the show.

In the first minute of extra time, a long ball gets inside the PSG penalty box where Suarez is trying to position himself to score. He is the ultimate shrewd forward, known for his theatrics in the penalty box, meaning he often fakes faults against him. Everyone knows. He is so mean and ruthless he once bit an Italian player in the World Cup.

A PSG defender running next him commits the ingenuity of touching him some. Suarez throws his arms in the air and goes down with a scream. I can see the play pretty well, and don't think this is an obvious foul. But the referee whistles and points to the penalty spot.

Surprisingly, since Messi had scored already the previous penalty kick for Barca, it's Neymar this time who steps up to take the great responsibility for the spot kick. A brief run-up, a bit of hesitation to see where the goalie may go, and then a perfect kick. Ball on the right side of the goal, goalie on the left. Neymar keeps his ran going, picks the ball from the back of the net, and sprints towards midfield.

We are all now standing up and cheering like mad. 5-1 Barca. An unbelievable tally before the game started. Now the numbers of goals are indeed 5 apiece for Barca and PSG, but PSG would still qualify given they have the precious away goal, which counts double.

Given what I've seen tonight, it does now seem a bit cruel to see Barca not qualify. They dominated this game. They are clearly superior. PSG are in complete disarray. But there are now less than 3 minutes left until truly time will run out. I'm still pessimistic Barca can do it. But... they scored two goals in the last 3-4 minutes, may be indeed this will be a fairy-tale night?

The game is really on now!!! The fans are going crazy. We all are looking at each other in disbelief. Is this really happening? Can Barca really do this? Is this real? Are we all dreaming?? Well, the big screen does say 5-1. And Barca is indeed still on the front foot, attacking now like mad.

Neymar is everywhere on the field. Tactical play is gone, now players are running everywhere, even defenders are attacking, all are switching positions, PSG has no more referring points, the coaches must be hating this, all that's driving play is adrenaline, pure passion for glory.

Neymar again gets the ball, this time in midfield. He dribbles forward, and then paints a soft ball towards the penalty spot. It seems way too far for most players, both Barca and PSG players, who are mostly positioned around the 18 yard line. But wait... there is Barca player madly running toward the flying ball... a PSG player is just behind him.

All happens in a flash. Sergi Roberto, a sub, number 20 for Barca, dives in the area with his right leg fully extended, and gets to the ball in midair. His kick redirects the ball towards the right side of the PSG goal, too far for the standing, incredulous PSG goalie. What a ball!! What a run!! Perhaps the most spectacular of all goals tonight!!!!!! 6-1!!!!!!!!!!!

The stadium now goes into delirium. Everyone is jumping up and down, hugging perfect strangers around them. The Barca players all start running with their arms up like maniacs, and quickly pile up in jubilation around the right corner kick area. I just cannot believe it. What a game!!

Soon after the ball is played again from center midfield, the referee whistles the end of this incredible duel. Barca scored its last goal with seconds to go, at the end of the 5<sup>th</sup> minute of extra time. A movie director could not have scripted this better. It's so true that life is so much better than any movie.

Now I do not ever want to leave Camp Nou. All are chanting. PSG players and fans disappear quickly. The Barca players go around the stadium jumping up and down in jubilation. Final score: 6-1. I've never seen a game live with more goals.

This will surely go down as one of the best games in history. Barcelona made Champions League history by becoming the first team to overturn a first-leg 4-0 deficit. They reached the quarter-finals for the 10th successive season. Wow.

The Barca players celebrate this amazing achievement for at least 15 minutes on the field, saluting their adoring fans. All chant Barca's hymn song in unison. I look at the stands, and, strangely, unusually for a match, nobody is leaving now. All are enjoying this 'extra-time' of pure joy.

I leave eventually, and go around the whole stadium not only to find the right way out – I'm by myself now – but also to enjoy the smiles and chants of all the fans as they slowly, almost unwillingly, leave the Camp Nou. I'm waving the two Barca flags I'll take back to Philadelphia – one for Andrea, one for Pietro.

I decide not to look for the private bus which should be waiting to take us back to the conference hotel, but instead to walk back. It's such a beautiful night, there are lots of people around, and I can burn some more calories and lots of adrenaline. I know I'll sleep even better.

**Thursday March 9th, 2017**

I wake up at 9am. I had a good night sleep, 8 hours. Probably not enough to recuperate fully from being awake over 30 of the prior 34 hours, but not bad… Shower, shave, white shirt, jacket, tie, and I'm a new man.

I have a quick breakfast in the posh hotel buffet, and I'm off to the Congress. In front of our hotel, the PSG soccer team bus. How sad these players must be. It's going to be a grim trip back to Paris for them.

I get in around 9:30 or so, and at the brake see Aaron Caughey, Chairman of Ob-Gyn at Oregon Health Science University in Portland, Oregon, a friend and a colleague I admire much. He is super nice. He agrees to write a chapter in one of the books I'm working on.

At 10am, there is the European Hyperglycemia in Pregnancy (HIP) declaration, quite a production. It is indeed a big deal most of the world has agreed based on science on similar criteria to diagnose gestational diabetes, and how to manage it.

The US unfortunately has different diagnostic criteria, and I'm doing my best to research this topic and hopefully align the US with the rest of the world (or viceversa, if the data shows otherwise). I'm always about the data, not about the politics or personalities.

From 11:10am to 12:40pm, Claudia, Daniele and I attend the Gestational Diabetes talks. With Claudia and our team at Jefferson we are indeed doing several studies on diabetes in pregnancy, and so we are very interested to hear the latest research and controversies.

We enjoy the first talks, by Fidelma Dunne from Galway in Ireland, Mary D'Alton from Columbia University in the USA, and Rosa Corcoy from Spain. I actually ask all three of them for their slides, something I do rarely, to make sure we have captured all their thoughts and wonderful information. They all agree, during their session, via their iPhones!! I guess we are all multitasking during these talks.

Moshe Hod gives a final push for global consensus regarding doing diabetes screening in pregnancy with the One Step, instead of the Two Step, which is more commonly done in the USA. I'm more than ever determined to do more research on this area; my biggest strength is being a learner, I always want to get to the bottom of an issue.

Then Daniele, Claudia and I hop on the Metro and go to the Liceu station with the L3 green line, which actually stops right here in Zona Universitaria.

We walk down La Rambla. It's my first taste of Barcelona. And what a delicious experience. La Rambla is the street in central Barcelona which connects Plaça de Catalunya with the Christopher Columbus Monument at Port Vell (see map on page 8). It's 1.2km long. La Rambla forms the boundary between the quarters of Barri Gòtic, to the east, and El Raval, to the west.

It's a beautiful day, perfect temperature in the upper 60's, sunny. La Rambla is crowded as usual with lots of young people, who seem to be all happy and smiling. While there are trees along this magnificent street, apart from the crowd one notices more the numerous outside restaurants and café' with people taking it easy, sitting down and enjoying delicious food and smooth drinks. This all happens in the central pedestrian sidewalk.

There are also countless souvenir kiosks, and shops, and newspaper stands. The crowd moves very slowly through this maze of wonderful options for entertainment. Very few if any are in a hurry. I think that it is a Thursday morning, which I usually spend closed in meetings (which I love, by the way). But this is not a bad alternative once in a while.

I try desperately to buy Marca, the Barcelona official daily sport newspaper, but it has been sold out everywhere. I end up buying with Daniele Mundo Deportivo, another Barcelona sport daily, which has a beautiful photo of Barca players celebrating, and a huge 'HEROES,' on its front page.

As the Spanish poet Federico García Lorca once said, La Rambla is 'the only street in the world which I wish would never end.' Daniele, Claudia and I have a great time. I'm glad we escaped from the Congress, even if briefly. We get to the beach, as La Rambla ends here – Rambla de Mar. This is Barceloneta.

I absolutely love the beach. I'm so happy now. I'm tempted to strip down and swim, but resist. I would make a mess of myself, and I'm sure the water is not that warm in March here. I'm getting wiser – or dummer, I'm not sure – in my later years. We take some photos. We relax and get a drink. Then we take the Metro back.

I get in the conference center around 4pm, in time to see Eduardo Fonseca, from Brazil, talk, which covers - to my surprise - a similar topic to the one I'll talk about at 5pm. He is a great guy; I've known and admired him for over 12 years. I'm sure I can entertain the audience anyway as I have a slightly different bent on several issues.

Today I have three talks, it's my busiest day. At 5pm, I co-chair a session with Montse Palacio, a great colleague from here in Barcelona. I'm supposed to start this session talking about the ultrasound assessment of the uterine cervix, which helps predicts preterm birth.

But first I have a bit of a surprise for Montse, who is from and lives and works in Barcelona. I start the session by waving the two Barcelona flags I brought from the game. And showing on the big screen the video I took at the end of the game. Everyone applauds. When you lecture, make sure you always start with something new, interesting, inspiring.

Montse speaks after me. Then a Mexican now in the USA, Edgar Hernandez-Andrade, and to follow him another Spanish researcher, Teresa Cobo. The final speaker of our session is my friend Bo Jacobsson from Sweden. Thankfully, for each of us there are a few questions. I'm so happy, this is always my favorite part, and where I'm at my best, and learn the most.

Overall we have a wonderful session. Miraculously, we finish on time at 6:27pm, a few minutes before the next session, at

6:30pm. May be not so miraculously: I'm also moderating the next session, which is in another Hall, so I had made sure all along to keep things on time ☺.

I get to Hall D with Mary D'Alton, the Chairman of Ob-Gyn at Columbia in New York, who co-chairs the next session with me. She talks, then me, then her again, the Gerry Visser from the Netherlands, then me again, then Yariv Yogev from Israel, then Gerry again, and finally Yariv again.

We each are supposed to speak for less than ten minutes each time, and we pretty much do so, even talking a few questions here and there and generating discussion. This session actually runs great, with a packed audience. We get lots of praises at the end. It's past 8pm when we end, I think we have earned dinner.

By bus, we get to the Congress VIP Dinner, which is in Liceu. I do not realize until we get there, but Liceu is the famous opera house right along La Rambla in Barcelona. I had noticed the building as perhaps the most beautiful along this street when we walked here earlier in the day.

In 1837, the Liceo Filodramático de Montesión (Philodramatic Lyceum of Montesión, now named Conservatori Superior de Música del Liceu) was founded in Barcelona to promote musical education (hence the name 'Liceo,' or lyceum) and to organize scenic representations of opera performed by Liceo students.

A theater was built in the convent building - named Teatro de Montesión or Teatro del Liceo de Montesión - and the first opera was Vicenzo Bellini's Norma (February 3rd, 1838). The repertoire was Italian, the most performed composers being Donizetti and Mercadante as well as Bellini and Rossini.

The building indeed stands out, and its 1847 façade is elegant, and now embellished by many flags, with the Catalan one in the middle. The main hall is grand, and we are received by gentlemen in white gloves offering us champagne. Not bad.

I chat with my many friends there. Jacob Bar from Israel and his wife. Some American colleagues. The Brazilian contingency.

Then Eduard Gratacos, the head of obstetrics in Barcelona, and a beautiful woman, who eventually I understand being his wife. Dinner is in a grand ballroom.

I'm lucky to sit with Gian Carlo Di Renzo, head of ob-gyn in Perugia Italy, and also the Secretary General of our international society, FIGO, who I think is the best organizer of conferences in our field. Next to me are Eduardo da Fonseca and his lovely young Brazilian wife. Fabio Facchinetti from University of Modena, and a few others are also at our table. Old friends, who I love to spend time with.

**Friday March 10th, 2017**

The plan for Friday is to visit as a tourist Barcelona as much as possible. And the way I like to sightsee is with guides. In Rick Steves' guide, which I borrowed from Andrea since he was here just last year, there are several free guided tours listed. I pick the Runner Bean tour, which has a Gaudí or an Old City tour at 11am.

Daniele and Claudia agree to join me, and I'm so happy. The weather today is supposed to be again in the low 70's and sunny: basically perfect. We get to the Metro, and we arrive soon along La Rambla. Our destination is Plaça Reial, where the tour is supposed to start from.

Plaça Reial means Royal Plaza, and is a square in the Barri Gòtic district of Barcelona. It's an elegant pedestrian plaza, with many restaurants and bars. We identify the free tour young staff, and sign up, deciding for the Gaudí tour. We are a bit early, so Daniele gets himself a coffee. I call my parents.

I must admit I do not know much about Gaudí, but every guide says basically that is architectural works are the best things to see in Barcelona. I also plan to come back tomorrow, or at least sometime in the future, and take the Old City tour, which is basically a tour of the main sites in Barcelona.

I figure one can do a tour of the city anytime, even by himself with a book guide or with local friends - I have a few -, but it would be absolutely impossible to learn about Gaudí and his works without a live guide.

Antoni Gaudí (June 25, 1852 - June 10, 1926) was a Catalan architect from Reus and the best known practitioner of Catalan Modernism. Gaudí's works reflect an individualized and distinctive style, really unique. Most of them are located in Barcelona, including his magnum opus, the Sagrada Família.

Gaudí's work was influenced by his three passions in life: architecture, nature, and religion. Gaudí considered every detail of his creations and integrated into his architecture such crafts as ceramics, stained glass, wrought ironwork forging and carpentry. He also introduced new techniques in the treatment of materials, such as trencadís which used waste ceramic pieces.

Under the influence of neo-Gothic art and Oriental techniques, Gaudí became part of the Modernista movement which was reaching its peak in the late 19th and early 20th centuries. His work transcended mainstream Modernisme, culminating in an organic style inspired by natural forms, such as trees, leaves, animals, etc. Gaudí rarely drew detailed plans of his works, instead preferring to create them as three-dimensional scale models and molding the details as he conceived them.

Gaudí's work enjoys global popularity and continuing admiration and study by architects. His masterpiece, the still-incomplete Sagrada Família, is the most-visited monument in Spain. Between 1984 and 2005, seven of his works were declared World Heritage Sites by UNESCO. Gaudí's Roman Catholic faith intensified during his life and religious images appear in many of his works. This earned him the nickname 'God's Architect' and led to calls for his beatification.

Our free guide is Jarrod, from Australia. I'm a bit surprised the guide is not a local, but soon Jarrod reveals himself to be not only a funny and entertaining guide, but also an expert guide, with excellent knowledge of everything Gaudí or Barcelona. He starts by telling us about... who else? Gaudí!

Antoni Gaudí was born in 1852 in Reus, to the coppersmith Francesc Gaudí i Serra and Antònia Cornet i Bertran. There is a bit of controversy regarding his birthplace, as he himself stated on various occasions that he was born in Riudoms, his paternal family's village. Jarrod always says Gaudí was from the province of Tarragona, where both Reus and Riudoms are. Tarragona is in Catalunya, which makes Gaudí a homeborn hero in Barcelona.

He was the youngest of five children. Have you ever read 'Born to rebel' by Frank Sulloway? It's a great book, that through scientific data explains how much birth order can influence our lives. Showing supporting data, he states that often first borns fulfill their parents dreams, and become doctors, lawyers, actors, professionals, etc.

As kids want to impress and be special to their parents' eyes, the second and the ones after usually choose something different that the previous siblings. If the first one became a lawyer, the second one could be an architect, the third perhaps an engineer, and the forth a doctor.

But as one gets later and later in the birth order, there is more freedom for the child to decide. The parents at some point run out of things they wish they had done. And give their 'later' children less direction, and therefore more freedom to decide for themselves, based on their interests and their strengths.

In fact, Sulloway makes several great examples of this. One that has stayed in my memory is that of a fifth of six children, who at the age of 22 was bold enough, courageous enough, curious enough, but especially free enough to take off on a boat for a five-year trip around the world. His name? Charles Darwin. It's amazing what one can accomplish when they are allowed to freely follow their passion.

So I'm not surprised Gaudí was the last of five children. He clearly pursued his own interests and his own special strengths. Gaudí had a deep appreciation for his native land and great pride in his Mediterranean heritage. He believed Mediterranean people to be endowed with creativity, originality and an innate sense for art and design.

Time spent outdoors, particularly during summer stays in the Gaudí family home Mas de la Calderera, afforded Gaudí the opportunity to study nature. Gaudí's enjoyment of the natural world led him to join the Centre Excursionista de Catalunya in 1879 at the age of 27. The organization arranged expeditions to explore Catalunya and southern France, often riding on horseback or walking ten kilometers a day.

As Jarrod states, young Gaudí suffered from poor health, including rheumatism, which may have contributed to his reticent and reserved character. These health concerns and the hygienist theories of Dr. Kneipp contributed to Gaudí's decision to adopt vegetarianism early in his life. His religious faith and strict vegetarianism led him to undertake several lengthy and severe fasts. These fasts were often unhealthy and occasionally, as in 1894, led to life-threatening illness.

Gaudí attended a nursery school run by Francesc Berenguer, whose son, also called Francesc, later became one of Gaudí's main assistants. He enrolled in the Piarists school in Reus where he displayed his artistic talents via drawings for a seminar called El Arlequín (the Harlequin).

During this time he worked as an apprentice in the Vapor Nou textile mill in Reus. In 1868 he moved to Barcelona to study teaching in the Convent del Carme. In his adolescent years Gaudí became interested in utopian socialism and, together with his fellow students Eduard Toda i Güell and Josep Ribera i Sans, planned a restoration of the Poblet Monastery that would have transformed it into a Utopian phalanstère.

Between 1875 and 1878, Gaudí completed his compulsory military service in the infantry regiment in Barcelona as a Military Administrator. Most of his service was spent on sick leave, enabling him to continue his studies. His poor health kept him from having to fight in the Third Carlist War, which lasted from 1872 to 1876.

In 1876 Gaudí's mother died at the age of 57, as did his 25-year-old brother Francesc, who had just graduated as a physician. During this time Gaudí studied architecture at the Llotja School and the Barcelona Higher School of Architecture, graduating in 1878.

To finance his studies, Gaudí worked as a draughtsman for various architects and constructors. In addition to his architecture classes, he studied French, history, economics, philosophy and aesthetics. His grades were average and he occasionally failed courses.

Jarrod recounts the story that, when handing him his degree, Elies Rogent, director of Barcelona Architecture School, said: 'We have given this academic title either to a fool or to a genius. Time will show.' Clearly time revealed he was a genius, as Jarrod implies, and as I will discover in the next two and a half hours on this tour.

We have been standing around Jarrod in Plaça Reial in front of an elegant street lamp. There is another exact one on the other side of the square. These lamps were designed by a young Gaudí, who was paid 12 euros for this job. They are not as extravagant as some of the later adult art by Gaudí, but nonetheless full of meaning, as all of Gaudí's works.

On top of the lamps, there is a symbol of Hermes, the Greek god, and the Barcelona flag. Jarrod also makes us notice that there is the English cross of St George on the lamp right in front of us. St George (Jordi in Catalan) is indeed also patron of Catalunya. On the lamp, there is also a motive for the Catalan flag.

The Catalan flag has a myth in itself, and a huge lore here and really around the world now. It dates back to the 11th century, and as such is one of the oldest flags in the world. It is made of five yellow and four red stripes. There is a famous legend about these red stripes.

Guifré el Pilós (Wilfred the Hairy) was the last count of Barcelona appointed by the Frankish kings, and the first to give as inheritance his domains, initiating the Dynasty Counts of Barcelona. The red four stripes on the yellow background were created after a battle against the Normans, when the Frankish king dipped his hand in an open wound of Guifré el Pilós, and then passed all four fingers above the golden shield of the Count of Barcelona.

With this act was created the shield of the House of Barcelona, symbol of the new sovereign conquered, and, over the years, these four red bloody stripes on a yellow background became the Catalan flag. This flag is called the Senyera (meaning 'flag' in Catalan), and is even the flag of the Italian city of Alghero, in Sardinia, in the past ruled by the Catalans.

A version of this Catalan flag is called Estelada, or starred flag, from 'estel,' meaning 'star.' The design of the Estelada comprises the red-and-yellow bars of the Senyera, with the addition of a five-pointed star in a triangle at the hoist. This unofficial flag is typically flown by Catalan separatists to express their support for an independent Catalunya. As all flags, a symbol often of human individualism and hatred. I've learned not to like flags much, as they are often used to divide people.

Jarrod states that Gaudí was a strong Catalan, very proud of his heritage. He refused to speak Spanish. He always lived in Catalunya, and the love of this region is clearly reciprocated with interest by his fellow modern Catalunyans.

Jarrod starts us on the walking tour. I'm delighted he is so knowledgeable, so passionate about his job, and so approachable. We start going by different houses made by Gaudí. Along the way, Jarrod explains to us that after his somewhat rebellious early years, Gaudí in his early 20's began to associate with classier people, and to dine in high class restaurants, in search of patrons for his works.

Casa Vicens is the first house Gaudí's designed. It is considered one of the first buildings of Art Nouveau. Casa Vicens was commissioned in 1877 by Manuel Vicens i Montaner, an owner of a brick and tile factory living in Barcelona at the time. He inherited this section of land from his mother on August 29, 1877, and hired the 25-year-old architect Antoni Gaudí for the project.

The style of Casa Vicens is a reflection of Neo-Mudéjar (Moorish) architecture, one of the popular styles that can be seen throughout Gaudí's architecture, including oriental and neoclassical as well. However, what was unique about Gaudí was that he mixed different styles together and incorporated a variety of different materials, such as iron, glass, ceramic tiles and concrete, many of which can be seen in this building, as Jarrod points out for us.

Gaudí broke away from tradition and created his new language of architecture, and Casa Vicens represents a new chapter in the history of Catalan architecture as well as the beginning of a successful career for Gaudí. Casa Vicens sold for 35 million last year.

Casa Vicens marks the first time Gaudí utilized an orientalist style, mixing together Hispano-Arabic inspiration. This was a style of architecture that completely broke with the norm of the period. This house marks therefore Gaudí's coming of age, being his first major work of architecture, and the beginning of an artistic revolution.

The next Gaudí's work we stop by is Palau Güell. Jarrod describes it from the narrow sidewalk in front of it, with us - about 20 people - lined against the wall, so to let pedestrians barely by. We are in the Carrer Nou de la Rambla, in the El Raval neighborhood of the city of Barcelona.

This mansion was commissioned to Antoni Gaudí by the industrial tycoon Eusebi Güell. It was built between 1886 and 1888. Eusebi Güell was at the time one of the wealthiest persons in the world, worth the equivalent of 70 billion currently. His fortune was made in textile. Jarrod points to his initials, EG, in cast iron on top of the main entrance.

Palau Güell became Güell's own residence. He moved in here in 1890, after its completion and decoration. He and his wife had ten children. The mansion is centered around the main room, in the first floor, for entertaining high society guests. Guests entered the home in horse-drawn carriages through the large front iron gates, which featured a parabolic arch and intricate patterns of forged ironwork resembling seaweed and in some parts a horsewhip, as we can admire.

Animals could be taken down a ramp and kept in the livery stable in the basement where the servants resided, while the guests went up the stairs to the receiving room. The ornate walls and ceilings of the receiving room disguised small viewing windows high on the walls where the owners of the home could view their guests from the upper floor and get a 'sneak peek' before greeting them, in case they needed to adjust their attire accordingly.

The main party room has a high ceiling with small holes near the top where lanterns were hung at night from the outside to give the appearance of a starlit sky. The house also has twenty chimneys, and lots of expensive amenities, especially if one considers this was built in the late 19th century.

Sadly, textile eventually became a less important trade, and Güell went bankrupt at the end of his life. His family eventually sold Palau Güell in 1938. Palau Güell though still stands to symbolize his grandiose times, and is now part of the UNESCO World Heritage Site 'Works of Antoni Gaudí.'

Jarrod guides us to Passeig de Gràcia via Metro L3, and the Green line. The metro here is clean, efficient, cheap. The part of Barcelona we are now in has large avenues, and is very elegant. I love it. The economic boom of the 1800s made this the area where the rich lived.

The architecture which became predominant during that period was the Art Nouveau, and Modernism. There were many ways of course to interpret this new art. Jarrod in fact recounts that we are in La Manzana de la Discordia, or The block (the 'apple' literally) of Discord. The discord was between architects.

La Manzana de la Discordia is the most famous collection of modernist buildings sharing the same façade in Barcelona. This is the block located in Passeig de Gràcia between calle Aragó and calle Consell de Cent, and it is a fine display of the contrasts between the different architectural trends of the day.

Jarrod shows us a few buildings next to each other here in Passeig de Gràcia. At number 35 is Casa Lleó Morera, designed by Domènech i Montaner; a little further along you come across Casa Amatller, designed by Puig i Cadafalch; and finally, Casa Batlló, the work by Gaudí.

The term Apple of Discord, or Manzana de la Discordia in Spanish, originates from the wedding between Peleus and Thetis in Greek mythology. All of the gods were invited to the wedding with the exception of Eris, the goddess of discord.

Despite this, Eris arrived at the wedding bearing a gift of a golden apple inscribed with the word kallisti, 'for the fairest.' Many of the goddesses fought to claim the apple, but Zeus brought an end to the violence by ordering Paris, the Prince of Troy, to select the fairest goddess. Paris eventually offered the apple to Aphrodite.

There are a number of similarities between this episode in Greek mythology and the existing rivalry among modernist architects and, in fact, the rivalry among their patrons to have the fairest building on the block on Passeig de Gràcia. As the word manzana can mean both city block and apple in Spanish, further parallels can be drawn between the Greek myth and Barcelona's architecture.

The building that is now Casa Batlló was built in 1877. It was a classical building without remarkable characteristics within the eclecticism traditional by the end of the 19th century. The building had a basement, a ground floor, four other floors and a garden in the back.

The house was bought by Josep Batlló in 1900. The design made the home undesirable to buyers but the Batlló family decided to buy the place due to its central, prestigious and fashionable location. It was an area where the prominent family could draw attention to themselves.

Josep Batlló chose the architect who had designed Park Güell because he wanted Gaudí to come up with a risky plan. Indeed Gaudí was not only by now renowned for his boldness, but had also transformed himself even more through the years. In fact, in 1894 Gaudí had gone missing, and started his religious fasts.

He never married, and went to church twice a day for most of his adult life. He became moody, grumpy. Gone were the fashionable clothes of his twenties and thirties. He was shaggy. The commission for this new work came when he was a desolate-looking 52 year old.

Casa Batlló was redesigned in 1904 by Gaudí. It took two years to finish it. The local name for the building is Casa dels

Ossos (House of Bones). I'll tell you soon why. As with other Gaudí's buildings, we do not go in, but admiring its façade and hearing Jarrod's detailed story is plenty of a thrill. This is perhaps the most amazing front of a house I've ever seen.

The façade has three distinct sections. The lower ground floor with the main floor and two first-floor galleries are contained in a structure of Montjuïc sandstone with undulating lines. The central part, which reaches the last floor, is a multicolored section with protruding balconies.

The top of the building is a crown. The roof's arched profile recalls the spine of a dragon with ceramic tiles for scales, and a small triangular window towards the right of the structure simulates the eye. Yes, I can see that! The tiles were given a metallic sheen to simulate the varying scales of the monster, with the color grading from green on the right side, where the head begins, to deep blue and violet in the center, to red and pink on the left side of the building.

A common theory about the building is that the rounded feature to the left of center, terminating at the top in a turret and cross, represents the lance of Saint George (patron saint of Catalunya, Gaudí's home), which has been plunged into the back of the dragon. There are indeed skulls and bones on the first floor front (hence the 'House of Bones' nickname for Casa Batlló), even if the impression of the building is anything but scary. It is inspiring, if anything.

The legend goes that the dragon ate one virgin a day. Thanks to the blood from the murdered virgins a rose grew - I can see the rose! The dragon and the princess married. Eventually the prince killed the dragon and saved the princess. The day of the dragon is still celebrated in Catalunya, on the 23rd of April, which is St George Day. Wow, what a story!

One of the highlights of the façade is a tower topped with a cross of four arms oriented to the cardinal directions. It is a bulbous, root-like structure that evokes plant life. There is a second bulb-shaped structure similarly reminiscent of a thalamus flower, which is represented by a cross with arms that are actually buds announcing the next flowering. Nature, religions, Gaudí's signatures and loves.

The tower is decorated with monograms of Jesus (JHS), Maria (M with the ducal crown) and Joseph (JHP), made of ceramic pieces that stand out golden on the green background that covers the façade. These symbols show again the deep religiosity of Gaudí, who was inspired by the contemporaneous construction of his basilica to choose the theme of the holy family.

The central part of the façade evokes the surface of a lake with water lilies, reminiscent of Monet's Nymphéas, with gentle ripples and reflections caused by the glass and ceramic mosaic. It is a great undulating surface covered with plaster fragments of colored glass discs combined with 330 rounds of polychrome pottery.

Above the central part of the façade is a smaller balcony, made of iron, with a different exterior aesthetic, closer to a local type of lily. Two iron arms were installed here to support a pulley to raise and lower furniture. There are also balconies with what look like carnival masks, and confetti seemingly coming down the walls of this incredible façade.

The façade of the main floor, made entirely in sandstone, is supported by two columns. The design is complemented by joinery windows set with multicolored stained glass. In front of the large windows, as if they were pillars that support the complex stone structure, there are six fine columns that seem to simulate the bones of a limb, with an apparent central articulation; in fact, this is a floral decoration.

The rounded shapes of the gaps and the lip-like edges carved into the stone surrounding them create a semblance of a fully open mouth, for which the Casa Batlló has been nicknamed the 'house of yawns.' The structure repeats on the first floor and in the design of two windows at the ends forming galleries, but on the large central window there are two balconies as described above.

The ground floor, in particular, has unusual tracery, irregular oval windows and flowing sculpted stone work. There are few straight lines, and much of the façade is decorated with a colorful mosaic made of broken ceramic tiles (trencadís). One last look at Casa Battló, and I completely agree that Gaudí was influenced by one of his younger artist friends, Salvador Dalí, one of my favorite painters.

The Batlló family lived on the Noble Floor of Casa Batlló until the middle of the 1950's. Then it was sold to the Bernaz family, owners of the Chupa Chups lollipop company. So Chupa Chups, which remind me always of Paola's ear lobes, are a Catalan product. Who knew.

Pere Mila and his wife Roser Segimon hired Gaudí in 1906 after he was done with Casa Batlló. Casa Milà is popularly known as La Pedrera (for 'open quarry'), given its unconventional rough-hewn appearance. It was the last private residence designed by Gaudí and was built between 1906 and 1910. It is at 92 Passeig de Gràcia, very close to Casa Batlló.

The façade is composed of large blocks of limestone from the Garraf Massif on the first floor and from the Villefranche quarry for the higher levels. The blocks were cut to follow the plot of the projection of the model, then raised to their location and adjusted to align in a continuous curve to the pieces around them.

Viewed from the outside, the building has three parts: the main body of the six-story blocks with winding stone floors; two floors set a block back with a different curve, similar to sea waves, of a smoother texture and whiter color, and with small holes that look like embrasures; and finally the body of the roof. The pillars are revolutionary.

Gaudí's original façade had some of its lower-level ironwork removed. In 1928, the tailor Mosella opened the first store in La Pedrera, and he eliminated the bars. This did not concern anyone, because in the middle of twentieth century, wrought ironwork had little importance. The ironwork was lost until a few years later, when Americans donated one of them to the MoMa, where it is on display.

There are 33 iron works on balconies. Each is original, Jarrod says. He points out that this masterpiece in some way started Abstract art years before Abstract art was ever invented. Gaudí was so revolutionary, so ahead of his times.

Jarrod also points to the written words on top of the building. Typical Gaudí, this is a prayer, stating with 'Arte Gratia ...' In the middle top of the façade, one can also see an iron 'M.' This is for Mila, the last name of the owners. There is also a Rose, for Roser who was Pere Mila's wife.

How many details would have I missed without a guide? Never travel again without following one. They are even free in many places!

With restoration initiatives launched in 1987, the façade was rejoined to some pieces of stone that had fallen. In order to respect the fidelity of the original, material was obtained from the Villefranche quarry, even though by then it was no longer operating. The attic has Gaudí's exhibition, which Jarrod suggest we come back to visit in the future.

The work of Gaudí on the rooftop of La Pedrera brought his experience at Palau Güell together with solutions that were clearly more innovative – this time creating shapes and volumes with more body, more prominence, and less polychromatic themes.

On the rooftop there are six skylights/staircase exits (four of which were covered with broken pottery and some that ended in a double cross typical of Gaudí), twenty-eight chimneys in several groupings, two half-hidden vents whose function is to renew the air in the building, and four domes that discharged to the façade. The staircases also house the water tanks; some of which are snail-shaped.

The stepped roof of La Pedrera is also called 'the garden of warriors,' by the poet Pere Gimferrer, because the amazing chimneys appear to be protecting the skylights. The huge sculptures are each a masterpiece. The character of Dark Wader was copied from Gaudí by the Star War director, George Lucas.

Some have also said that La Pedrera's top has been modeled after mountains in Cappadocia, Turkey. The Rooftop terrace is supposed to be unbelievable. It has undergone a radical restoration, removing chimneys added in interventions after Gaudí, television antennas, and other elements that degraded the space.

The restoration brought back the splendor to the chimneys and the skylights that were covered with fragments of marble and broken Valencia tiles. One of the chimneys was topped with glass pieces – it was said that Gaudí did that the day after the inauguration of the building, taking advantage of the empty bottles from the party.

It was restored with the bases of champagne bottles from the early twentieth century. The repair work has enabled the restoration of the original impact of the overhangs made of stone from Ulldecona with fragments of tiles. This whole set is more colorful than the façade, although here the creamy tones are dominant.

The building was controversial because of its undulating stone façade, twisting wrought iron balconies and windows designed by Josep Maria Jujol. Several structural innovations include a self-supporting stone front, columns and floors free of load-bearing walls, an underground garage and sculptural elements on the roof.

The construction of the building, as many of Gaudí's works, eventually went over budget. Jarrod explains that Rosario Sagimon, who was the mistress of Mr. Mila, eventually ended up paying a lot of Pedrata.

La Pedrata was the first masterpiece recognized to Gaudí. In 1984, it was declared a World Heritage Site by UNESCO. It is currently the headquarters of the Fundació Catalunya-La Pedrera which manages exhibitions and other activities at Casa Milà.

Claudia, Daniele and I, as well as the rest of the group, get into another Metro, and in two stops we are, magically, at the

Sagrata Família. The metro leaves us right nearby it, so that one, coming out of the underground, is immediately impressed by this huge, unique structure.

The Basílica i Temple Expiatori de la Sagrada Família is a Roman Catholic church, and the biggest attraction in Barcelona. Construction began in 1882 under architect Francisco Paula de Villar, who resigned in 1883.

Taking over the project, Gaudí, then 31, transformed it with his architectural and engineering style, combining Gothic and curvilinear Art Nouveau forms. Gaudí devoted most of his life to the project, and at the time of his death at age 73 in 1926, less than a quarter of the project was complete.

Sagrada Família's construction progressed slowly, as it relied on private donations (Jarrod says 'of sinners') and was interrupted by the Spanish Civil War, only to resume intermittent progress in the 1950s. Construction passed the midpoint in 2010 with some of the project's greatest challenges remaining and an anticipated completion date of 2026, the centenary of Gaudí's death.

The basílica has a long history of dividing the citizens of Barcelona: over the initial possibility it might compete with Barcelona's cathedral, over Gaudí's design itself, over the possibility that work after Gaudí's death disregarded his design, and the 2007 proposal to build an underground tunnel of Spain's high-speed rail link to France which could disturb its stability.

The metro has left us closest to the Nativity façade. We go around the beautiful park in front, to stare at this incredible front from its middle. Jarrod starts by saying that Gaudí left a lot of models and drawings. The completed model has three façades: this Nativity, facing East; the Passion and death, facing West; and the Glory and ascension into heaven, facing South. So much symbolism.

The models also have lots of towers, only some of which have been completed. Jarrod points to the Tower of the Virgin Mary, currently one of the most prominent. The massive tower of Jesus, still not finished, will be an incredible 170 meters (558 feet) high. This was designed to be one meter lower than Montjuic, the tallest hill around Barcelona, to respect nature.

Constructed between 1894 and 1930, the Nativity façade was the first façade to be completed. Such, it bears the most direct Gaudí influence. Dedicated to the birth of Jesus, it is decorated with scenes reminiscent of elements of life. Characteristic of Gaudí's real-life style, the sculptures are ornately arranged and decorated with scenes and images from nature, each a symbol in their own manner.

For instance, the three porticos are separated by two large columns, and at the base of each lies a turtle or a tortoise (one to represent the land and the other the sea; each are symbols of time as something set in stone and unchangeable). In contrast to the turtle figures and their symbolism, two chameleons can be found at either side of the façade, and are symbolic of change.

The façade faces the rising sun to the East, a symbol for the birth of Christ. It is divided into three porticos, each of which represents a theological virtue: Hope on the left, Faith on the right, and Charity in the middle. Four towers complete the façade and are each dedicated to a Saint (Matthias the Apostle, Saint Barnabas, Jude the Apostle, and Simon the Zealot).

Jarrod points to so many details of this masterpiece, but it's hard for me to keep track of all he is saying. There is so much detail! He points to Mary sitting on a donkeys, and people fleeting to Egypt. Then to Herod and a soldier killing a baby. The babies are skinny babies.

There are also many animals in this huge setting. Gaudí loved animals. He never ate meat. The casting of animals was apparently very difficult. Jarrod points to the scene with the Holy family in main entrance. This is the portal of Charity. One can see the Virgin Mary, Joseph, Jesus, then the ox and the ass, the three wise men on the left, and three adoring shepherds on the right.

Above them all, there is the Shooting Christmas Star, and also angels without wings to announce the event. Jarrod also points to the huge cypress tree on the very top of the façade, and a bridge behind it. This Tree of Life rises above the door of Jesus in the portico of Charity.

Originally, Gaudí intended for this façade to be polychromed, for each archivolt to be decorated with a wide array of colors. He wanted every statue and figure to be painted. In this way the human figures would appear as alive as the figures of plants and animals.

Gaudí chose this façade to embody the structure and decoration of the whole church. He was well aware that he would not finish the church and that he would need to set an artistic and architectural example for others to follow. He also chose for this façade to be the first on which to begin construction and for it to be, in his opinion, the most attractive and accessible to the public.

He believed that if he had begun construction with the Passion Façade, one that would be hard and bare (as if made of bones), before the Nativity Façade, people would have withdrawn at the sight of it.

Work on the Sagrada Família stopped in 1935, and did not start back until 1950. Some of the statues were destroyed in 1936, and subsequently reconstructed by the sculptor Sotoo.

The Glory façade has been built only since 2002. Eventually, it will be the largest and most monumental of the three façades and will represent one's ascension to God. It will also depict various scenes such as Hell, Purgatory, and will include elements such as the Seven Deadly Sins and the Seven Heavenly Virtues.

It was started with sandstone, but Jarrod says the quarry finished so now they are utilizing reused sandstone. This Glory façade is currently not impressive yet. But it will be eventually the main entrance, and given prominence by a huge park in front.

Now, where the park will be, there are lots of busy buildings, which will need to be bought. The completion of this façade will require the demolition of two complete blocks full of buildings across the Carrer de Mallorca.

This principal façade will offer access to the central nave. Dedicated to the Celestial Glory of Jesus, it will represent the road to God: Death, Final Judgment, and Glory, while Hell is left for those who deviate from God's will.

Aware that he would not live long enough to see this façade completed, Gaudí made a model which was demolished in 1936, whose original fragments were the base for the development of the design for the façade.

To reach the Glory Portico the large staircase will lead over the underground passage built over Carrer de Mallorca with the decoration representing Hell and Vice. It will be decorated with demons, idols, false gods, heresy and schisms. Purgatory and death will also be depicted, the latter using tombs along the ground.

The portico will have seven large columns dedicated to spiritual gifts. At the base of the columns there will be representations of the Seven Deadly Sins, and at the top, The Seven Heavenly Virtues.

The Passion façade was built according to the design that Gaudí created in 1917. The construction began in 1954, and the towers, built over the elliptical plan, were finished in 1976. It is especially striking for its spare, gaunt, tormented characters, including emaciated figures of Christ being scourged at the pillar; and Christ on the Cross. These controversial designs are the work of Josep Maria Subirachs.

In 1911, Gaudí had Maltese fever. This disease, also called Brucellosis, is a highly contagious zoonosis caused by ingestion of unpasteurized milk or undercooked meat from infected animals, or close contact with their secretions. It is no surprise that Gaudí, with his love of animals, contracted this condition. Brucella are small bacteria that function as facultative intracellular parasites, causing chronic disease, which usually persists for life.

Gaudí then stayed for a time in Puigcerda, where his condition worsened and, believing his time had come, he made out his will. To the day of his death, he worked exclusively on the

Sagrada Família, and in 1925 moved his residence to the studio he had on the premises.

The fact that Gaudí was suffering when he designed the Passion façade is obvious in its current rendering. This façade is somber, and haunting. The main entrance is ornate with enormous Sequoia trees. The theme is the last days of Jesus' life.

In contrast to the highly decorated Nativity Façade, the Passion Façade is austere, plain and simple, with ample bare stone, and is carved with harsh straight lines to resemble the bones of a skeleton. Dedicated to the Passion of Christ, the suffering of Jesus during his crucifixion, the façade was intended to portray the sins of man.

In 1987 a team of sculptors, headed by Josep Maria Subirachs, began work sculpting the various scenes and details of the façade. They aimed to give it a rigid, angular form to provoke a dramatic effect.

Gaudí intended for this façade to strike fear into the onlooker. He wanted to 'break' arcs and 'cut' columns, and to use the effect of chiaroscuro (dark angular shadows contrasted by harsh rigid light) to further show the severity and brutality of Christ's sacrifice.

Facing the setting sun, indicative and symbolic of the death of Christ, the Passion Façade is supported by six large and inclined columns, designed to resemble sequoia trunks. Above there is a pyramidal pediment, made up of eighteen bone-shaped columns, which culminate in a large cross with a crown of thorns.

Each of the four towers is dedicated to an apostle (James, Thomas, Philip, or Bartholomew) and, like the Nativity Façade, there are three porticos, each representing the theological virtues, though in a much different light.

The scenes sculpted into the façade may be divided into three levels, which ascend in an S form and reproduce the Via Crucis of Christ. The lowest level depicts scenes from Jesus' last night before the crucifixion, including the Last Supper, the Kiss of Judas, Ecce Homo, and the Sanhedrin Trial of Jesus. Jarrod points to the last supper. There is the statue of an old man in middle: it's the old Gaudí! The profile is easily recognizable.

The middle level portrays the Calvary, or Golgotha, of Christ, and includes The Three Marys, Saint Longinus, Saint Veronica, and a hollow-face illusion of Christ on the Veil of Veronica.

In the third and final level, the Death, Burial and Resurrection of Christ can be seen. A bronze figure situated on a bridge creating a link between the towers of Saint Bartholomew and Saint Thomas represents the Ascension of Jesus.

While the Nativity façade is indeed a spectacular work of art, this Passion façade leaves even more of a strong impression deep inside. It's truly magnificent in its striking graveness. I feel somber inside.

Jarrod then goes on to recount the last few days of Gaudí's life. On June 7, 1926, he was run over by a tram at the intersection of Carrer de Bailén and the Gran Vía. In his old age, Gaudí was a man who conformed with little and dressed without much care; so much so that the day of his accident nobody recognized him as he lay on the ground.

He did not seek out contact with journalists and he avoided cameras, so there were few photographs of the architect. The taxi drivers refused to take a poor vagabond to the hospital. Gaudí died of the consequences of the severe injuries from being hit by the tram at the age of 74, on June 12, 1926.

If it hadn't been for the tram he may have lived many more years, since his father had lived to the age of 93, with all his vigor. Half of Barcelona dressed in black to give final homage to a man that had become very popular, although few had ever met him personally. His body was buried in the crypt of the edifice where he had worked for the last 43 years of his life, the Sagrada Família.

Jarrod is done with his magnificent tour. I tip him generously, as he has been superb. I'm sad it's over. Claudia, Daniele and I then decide on a place to eat, as it's almost 2pm. At

3pm we have booked a guided tour of the inside of Sagrada Família. Our plans are progressing perfectly.

We decide to get paellas in a small inelegant restaurant right across Glory façade. As we wait for our food, I step outside and talk and video for a while with my mamma and papa'. I also catch my brother Michele via a WhatsApp call in the Maldives, where he is vacationing. Today's is his birthday! Hard to believe I have a 48 year old younger brother.

We get to the entrance of the Nativity façade part of Sagrata Família 15 minutes before the 3pm scheduled tour, and find the spot from where the tour will start from. I spot Jacob Bar's wife, who greets me warmly. They have also booked the same tour! Jacob arrives after a few more minutes.

The tour guide is a young woman, very good but to me a bit less organized and entertaining than Jarrod. She starts by telling us that the construction of Sagrata Família started in 1882, with Gaudí taking over a year later. He gave the inside of the building more natural light, and created a forest inside.

After Gaudí finished La Pedrata in 1912, he only worked for the rest of his life on the Sagrata Família, his life masterpiece. The guide states, to my surprise, that the Sagrata Família is the second most visited site in Barcelona, with Parc Güell at number one. I'm glad tomorrow I have a chance to visit Parc Güell, hopefully. The most visited museum in Barcelona is the Barca FC museum, the museum of Barcelona's famed soccer team.

Outside this Nativity entrance, the guide shows us the palm trees, and the sculpted animals everywhere. She points to the four bell towers in the Nativity façade, and then she explains on a model how the Glory façade will eventually look like.

She shows us the four big towers for the evangelists, and the model of the 170 meters highest tower still to be constructed. This tower will make La Sagrada Família the highest church in the world. Eventually there will be 18 towers, with 10 more towers needed to be built.

She also points out that the columns in this Nativity façade are palm trees, and the sea the Mediterranean Sea. That the cypress tree is holy in Spain. That the choir has Japanese characters. In the right ride of the Nativity façade, she shows us St Joseph the grinder, and some amazing snow which seems to be melting, marvelously rendered from sandstone.

The guide now takes us inside. On the door, she makes us notice twenty different super-detailed insects sculpted all along the tall structure. La Sagrada Família is unlike any other church or monument I've ever seen also in the inside, not only in the magnificent façades.

First of all, the light is different. It's pretty much 100% natural light. It feels as if we are in a forest. There are 52 columns (same number as the weeks in a year) which are shaped as huge trees, with branches on top.

It's interesting what materials were used. Sandstone was used for the oldest parts of this church, like the Nativity façade, the basement and the crypt. Then in 1920 another solution was needed because sandstone was found to be too soft to sustain this massive building.

So Gaudí created a skeleton to support his plans. Therefore the main columns are made of porphyry from Iran. This is the second hardest stone after diamond. These columns are indeed a unique Gaudí design. Besides branching to support their load, their ever-changing surfaces are the result of the intersection of various geometric forms.

The simplest example is that of a square base evolving into an octagon as the column rises, then a sixteen-sided form, and eventually to a circle. This effect is the result of a three-dimensional intersection of helicoidal columns (for example a square cross-section column twisting clockwise and a similar one twisting counter-clockwise).

The church plan is that of a Latin cross with five aisles. The central nave vaults reach forty-five meters (150 feet) while the side nave vaults reach thirty meters (100 feet). The transept has three aisles. The columns are on a 7.5 meter (25 feet) grid. However, the columns of the apse, resting on del Villar's foundation, do not adhere to the grid, requiring a section of columns of the ambulatory to transition to the grid thus creating a horseshoe pattern to the layout of those columns.

The crossing rests on the four central columns of porphyry supporting a great hyperboloid surrounded by two rings of twelve hyperboloids (currently under construction). The central vault reaches sixty meters (200 feet). The apse is capped by a hyperboloid vault reaching seventy-five meters (250 feet). Gaudí intended that a visitor standing at the main entrance be able to see the vaults of the nave, crossing, and apse; thus the graduated increase in vault loft.

Branching out high up on the four central columns, Gaudí placed big modern statues which are leaning in towards the very center of the church, almost like they are looking down and surveilling the church-goes below. There are clearly labeled each with the name of one of the four evangelists: Matthew, Mark, Luke and John.

Interestingly, none of the interior surfaces are flat; the ornamentation is comprehensive and rich, consisting in large part of abstract shapes which combine smooth curves and jagged points. Even detail-level work such as the iron railings for balconies and stairways are full of curvaceous elaboration.

The guide points and describes next the central canopy with a sculpture holding Jesus. The grapes hanging from the canopy are made of Murano glass. We walk then to our left, towards the Glory façade side. What's most spectacular here is the tainted huge windows on both the East and West side of this part of the church.

The Nativity (East) side windows are full of greens and blues. This is the side where the sun rises. But at this time of day even more impressive are those in the Passion (West) side. The intensity of the red and orangey hues is startling with the low afternoon light. These color themes are one of my favorite parts of this masterpiece. The Glory façade glass is not colored yet.

The total capacity of this enormous church is said to be 9,000 people. The guide states that over 2,500 can be here in the ground floor. And that in the balcony where the choir is more than 1,200 can be easily accommodated. She shows us some glass near the floor, which is put there so one can take selfies with the beautiful ceiling above. This must have been done before iPhone came out with reverse view on their cameras...

In this part of the church, near the Glory façade, there is a big dark wall with the 'Our Father' prayer in Catalan. There is also a St George sculpture, done by the same sculptor as the outside statues. The guide then goes on to explain the many symbolisms of this structure.

She states that there are exactly 7.5 meters between columns. There are 15 meters between other structures. The columns are 30 meters high. The tallest tower will be 172.5 meters. All these numbers are multiples of 7.5. Legend states that 7 is the number for imperfection, while 8 is the number for heaven. So 7.5 is the meeting point between man and God. What a great story! But apparently Gaudí left no written explanation for any of this.

The guide then takes us outside, to describe the Passion façade, which we had already reviewed in details with Jarrod. She walks our eyes first to the left where the last supper is. She points to Judas' kiss with the snake nearby. Then to the scene of the Cross and veil. Then on the right to St Peter's denial. There are three ladies and the rooster, to signify the three refusals.

There are scenes of Jesus dying on cross, carving the cross, and falling down three times carrying the cross. Veronica's towel is depicted, next to her Roman soldiers. The guide then shows us the old man who is Gaudí. She goes on to recount his strange death, after being run over by a train.

He was not recognized, and mistaken for a homeless. He was found in the hospital two days after by Sagrata Família workers who were surprised he did not show up at work. What a strange, cruel faith life reserves for us humans sometimes.

Gaudí left plenty of directions on how to finish his beloved Sagrata Família. Unfortunately a big fire in Barcelona in 1936 destroyed many of his papers, but the plaster models remained. Not all his plans will be able to become reality though. The guide states that, for example, the Glory façade is impossible to build as Gaudí wanted.

Our last stop is the exhibition down below inside La Sagrada Família. There are models from Gaudí and also from the other one hundred architects who have contributed to this magnificent building. The Gaudí models are of course handmade, while now 3D printers are used.

The guide describes for us in particular a large Gaudí model of the whole church. She shows how Gaudí made calculations from this model. The model is actually upside down, and mirrors help to make sense of it. Fascinating how ingenious Gaudí was. The guide ends the tour stating that the annual income from tickets at La Sagrata Família is about 60 million euros, and that 25 of these are used for construction.

What an amazing wonder of the world La Sagrada Família is. I had heard about it all my life, but reality in this case beats expectations. Describing Sagrada Família, art critic Rainer Zerbst said, 'It is probably impossible to find a church building anything like it in the entire history of art.' I agree.

Gaudí's work on the building is part of a UNESCO World Heritage Site, and in November 2010 Pope Benedict XVI consecrated and proclaimed it a minor basilica distinct from a cathedral, which must be the seat of a bishop.

By about 5:20pm we are back in the congress. At 6pm, I'm again moderating a session and also speaking during it. In Hall A, the main hall, I catch the end of the talk of a German colleague, then a Spanish colleague speaks, and then I hear what I think was the most intriguing talk of the whole congress, by Basky Thilaganathan from St George's in London in the UK.

Basky is always an inspiring speaker. That is I think the most important characteristic of a good talk. He also has a great quote in his talk: 'When an honest man is mistaken, he will either cease to be honest, or he will accept to be mistaken.' So true.

In our session at 6pm, I moderate this time with Moshe Hod, the organizer of the whole conference, and get him a deserved applause. The theme is again SMFM (the USA) meets DIP (Europe). Mary D'Alton talks about steroids after 34 weeks, I talk about universal cervical length screening in low-risk women, then an Israeli on hypothyroidism in pregnancy and baby's IQ, Bo Jacobsson on progesterone for preterm birth, an Australian on gestational diabetes, Eduard Gratacos on preeclampsia and aspirin, and Francesc Figueras on how to identify the at risk fetus at term. It all goes well.

Then we go to the BarNatal Hospital with Montse Palacio, Edgar Hernandez-Andrade, and Nir Melamed from Israel but now working in Canada, and others. Montse is simply so nice. She takes us on her family van. I sit next to her and find out some more how wonderful she is. As I said, she is from Barcelona, and lives and works here.

I knew she was a great professional, and had published some great research. She had also been supercollaborative on common important projects. So altruistic and hardworking. I now discover also that she has a thriving family life, wonderful kids (one in the US playing basketball in college!). Her sparkly blue eyes project her enthusiasm for life. I highly admire her.

The visit to her hospital is very interesting. They do a lot of deliveries, practice excellent medicine, and I meet an army of their researchers, many from all over the world, especially the Spanish speaking world, but not only. All young, eager, fertile minds ready to discover the next best thing in preeclampsia, preterm birth, the placenta, labor, or fetal or maternal diseases. Wow. I'm impressed.

At the end of this eye-opening hospital tour, I have to make a decision regarding three possibilities for dinner. There is an official congress dinner. Montse invites me to join her Barcelona team who is having dinner with Eduard Gratacos, their leader, and the many other members of their team I've just met these last couple of days.

I chose the option I had arranged for before I was aware of these other choices. I'll join Ilaria Bianchi, an ob-gyn physician from Florence, Italy, who spent many months with us at Jefferson in Philadelphia a few years ago, and now lives and works successfully here in Barcelona. Daniele instead decides to go with his sister, who lives here, while Claudia joins me.

We have dinner at a great tapas place. The company is interesting. Apart from me, Ilaria, and Claudia, we are joined by Tilde D'Amico, an Italian-American from Philadelphia friend with Ilaria, and by her coworker who we call 'Harley Davidson,' as this is how her name sounds like.

We eat lots of taps prepared in dozens of different ways, and a good amount of sangria. I text Montse during dinner to make sure she was not offended I did not join her, and to see if maybe I can join her a bit later. She does not see my WhatsApp; probably better this way, I always try to please too many and to do too much.

In great company, we stay until midnight, then I take a taxi back to the hotel by myself, and during it call Paola, to check in on each other's lives.

**Saturday March 11th, 2017**


I have to unfortunately set the alarm clock for 7:15am. I am due in the conference hall by 8am for the last session I have a talk in. It runs from 8am until 9:30am in hall C. I'm so lucky as the session is with friends, moderated by Eduardo Fonseca from Brazil and Maria Goya from here in Barcelona. They are also the first speakers, followed by me, and then Montse Palacio again from here in Barcelona. We are all Latinos!

The session is over at 9:30am, I answer a few more questions from audience attendees, and say hello to other colleagues in the ensuing break. Then I go change quickly to more comfortable clothes in my hotel a block away, and, rejoined by Daniele and Claudia, we head again to Plaça Reial and a new free Barcelona tour! I'm so excited!

It's again a beautiful gorgeous day. How can I be so lucky? Once in Plaça Reial, we sign up this time for the Barri Gòtic tour, or the tour of the Gothic quarter, which is basically the Old City, downtown, directly on the left side of La Rambla if one is looking towards the Mediterranean (see map on page 8).

Jarrod is around, and greets us warmly. We are initially assigned to another guide, but to our delight eventually it's Jarrod who comes over and says that, since there are so many people today, they switched things around, made smaller groups, and he will be our guide today too!! Yes!!!

He starts by giving us some general information about Barcelona and Catalunya. In Spain, there are four major languages. One is Castellano, the official 'Madrid' language. Then there is Catalan, spoken here. Gallego is spoken in the north-west, and has similarities with Portuguese. Then there is Basque, a strange (as said by Jarrod) language with no linguistic relatives spoken in the north-east of Spain.

There are a few versions about how Barcelona was founded. Option 1 is that in 15 BC Augustus' soldiers founded it. The original settlement is from before, as in the 3rd and 2nd centuries BC, the area was settled by the Laietani, an Iberian people, at Barkeno on the Táber hill (present-day Ciutat Vella, or 'Old City') and at Laie, believed to have been located on Montjuïc.

The area then fell to Carthaginian control, but later the Romans set out to conquer the whole of the Iberian peninsula in the Cantabrian Wars, a conquest which was declared complete by Augustus in 19 BC. Barcelona (Barcino) was then considerably less important than the major centers of Tarraco (Tarragon), which is modern day Tarragona, and Caesaraugusta, known today as Zaragoza.

Option 2 is a lot more mythological, and attributes the foundation of the city to Hercules before the foundation of Rome. During the fourth of his Labors, Hercules joined Jason and the Argonauts in search of the Golden Fleece, travelling across the Mediterranean in nine ships.

One of the ships is lost in a storm off the Catalan coast, and Hercules sets out to locate it. He finds it wrecked by a small hill (modern Mountjuic), but with the crew saved. The crew is so taken by the beauty of the location that they found a city with the name Barca Nona ('Ninth Ship').

While this second option is so much more appealing, it is made up, says Jarrod, while option 1 is true. I read later that another legend credits the Carthaginian general Hamilcar Barca, father of Hannibal, with the foundation of Barcelona around 230 BC, giving it the name Barkenon. Despite the similarities between the name of this Carthaginian family and that of the modern city, it is usually accepted that the origin of the name 'Barcelona' comes from the Iberian word 'Barcino,' or 'Barkeno.'

Barrod goes on to describe the fact that there were walls surrounding the newly founded city of Barcelona. Plaça Reial was made in the 19th century. A convent was demolished to make this square. It was built in celebration of the discovery of America, and dedicated to King Ferdinand VII.

We take off touring with Jarrod. It's a small group, we can hear Jarrod great. He takes us next to another square nearby in Barri Gòtic. Under the watchful eye of the stunning church Santa Maria del Pi, Plaça del Pi is a charming square with an authentic bohemian atmosphere.

Plaça del Pi is located at the end of the street Petritxol, just off the Rambla. The square is surrounded by old decorated façades, antique shops, bars and restaurants with interesting cuisine. Its translation (pi) means 'eternal pine' and is so named because when the square was opened there was a large pine tree in the middle, which had to be replaced but the new one is still there.

Jarrod lets us admire the huge mural graffiti in the building on the opposite side of the church. There is also a nice little market dedicated to artisan products. Jarrod gives a few free minutes. With Daniele, we visit the inside of the main church, Santa Maria del Pi, with its huge and famous multicolored rose window. Jarrod explains to us that the Catalan style is a gothic made simpler. We then also shop in the open market, where I get some cheeses for Paola and the family.

At the start of the 5th century, the Western Roman Empire suffered more serious attacks at the hands of various Germanic peoples. Ataulf led the Visigoths into southern Gaul, and after a defeat at the hands of the Roman forces at Narbona (modern Narbonne) in 414, moved across the Pyrenees into the Tarraconensis (the province where Barcelona had become now a major city). Ataulf in fact established his court at Barcino, where he was murdered by one of his own troops in 415.

Barcino would remain an important, if provincial, center of the Visigoth kingdom, notably because of its excellent defensive walls. The language spoken at the time was undoubtedly Vulgar Latin, including by the Visigoth rulers who were rapidly latinized.

Over time, the spelling of the Latin Barcino (declined as Barcinone, Barcinonem, Barcinonam, Barcinona) gradually came to include an intercalated 'h' to represent the hard 'k' sound (as in modern Italian), and the use of the different Latin cases declined.

The Jewish population of Barcino/Barchinona dates from the mid-4th century at the latest. While the Jewish religion had been tolerated by the Romans, Jews suffered varying degrees of discrimination and persecution under the Visigoths. Visigoth King Recceswinth outlawed many essential Jewish practices, including circumcision of males, dietary laws (kosher), marriage laws and ceremonies, and the celebration of Passover.

Jarrod explains to us in fact that we are in the oldest quarters in Barcelona, and in front to the oldest house, still standing from these early medieval times. It is a Jewish house, in Career de la Fruita, a very small alley.

Records indicate that four synagogues existed in Barcelona in the 14th century. Of these, only the Sinagoga Mayor has been found, reclaimed, and restored. Jarrod explains that there was indeed a very old synagogue in the corner we are in, facing south-east towards Jerusalem.

The original synagogue dates back perhaps to as early as the 3rd or 4th century. Jarrod points to the inscriptions in Hebrew on the wall. Up to the 12th century Jewish people were doing well. They were mostly money lenders.

This site was in medieval times a kind of a city within a city, called 'El Call.' The meaning of this could be either the Hebrew word for 'congregation,' or maybe from 'calle,' or 'narrow street.' There were back then 4,000 Jews in Barcelona, or 10% of its population.

But in the beginning 13th century anti-Jewish feelings started. The Black Death of 1348-1351 killed 50% of Barcelona's population. The Jewish were accused of poisoning the wells and causing the Bubonic Plague. In 1391 Jewish were murdered if they did not agree to convert to Christianity. In 1492 the Jews of Barcelona were finally expelled.

For years, the building where the holy site once was served many functions, except that of a synagogue. In the late 17th century, apartments were built on top of the structure. In the late 20th century, a study on the El Call area led to the rediscovery of the synagogue, its subsequent purchase in 1995 by a Jewish association, its management by the Call Association of Barcelona (founded in 1997 to support the synagogue recovery project) and its careful restoration. It is now back to being an official synagogue.

Excavations during the 20th century revealed a foundation and Roman wall structure dating back to the reign of Emperor Caracalla, who, in 212 had granted full Roman citizenship to the Jews of the empire. This synagogue is believed to be is one of the oldest in Europe.

Moorish forces (Muslims from North Africa) arrived in the Iberian peninsula in 711. After the conquest and devastation of Tarraco in 717, 'Barchinona' surrendered peacefully and was hence spared from major destruction. While the cathedral was converted into a mosque and taxes levied on non-Muslims, religious freedom and civil government was largely respected. Muslim rule in Barcelona lasted roughly 85 years.

Louis the Pious, son of Charlemagne, captured Barcelona in 801 after a siege of several months. The first Carolingian Counts of Barcelona were little more than royal administrators, but the position steadily gained in power and independence from the central rule with the weakening of the Carolingian kings.

The last Count of Barcelona to be appointed by the Carolingian authorities was Wilfred the Hairy in 878. He is considered the first Catalonian king. As we have seen in page 34, the Carolingian king Charles the Bald rewarded his bravery in battle against the Normans by giving him a coat of arms. The king slid Wilfred's blood-stained fingers over a copper shield, and thus was the Catalan flag Senyera first born.

At his death in 897, Wilfred's possessions were divided between his sons Wilfred II Borrel, Sunyer and Miró the Younger, marking the beginning of a hereditary regime. In 988, Wilfred II Borrell Count of Barcelona denied to continue to pledge fidelity to the Carolingian court. This is considered the first independence date of Cataluña. The city of Barcelona, easily defensible and with excellent fortifications, prospered with the increasing power of its overlords.

We get to the Plaça de Sant Jaume (Saint James's Square), a square at the center of the Old City of Barcelona and the administrative heart of both the city and surrounding Catalunya. Both the Palace of the Generalitat of Catalunya and the City Hall are located here across from one another.

The Plaça Sant Jaume is located at the former center of the Roman city of Barcino, where its main streets, the Cardo (modern day Llibreteria and Call streets) and Decumanus (now the streets of Bisbe/Ciutat/Regomir), crossed. At this junction there was the forum and the Temple of Augustus, of which four columns are preserved on top of Mont Tàber, found at the adjacent Paradís Street.

The Square takes its modern name from the Church of Sant Jaume, which had been located at the site of the square since medieval times. Formerly, the city council of Barcelona met in the porch at the front of that church, until it bought a number of nearby homes that would house the future headquarters of the institution on the neighboring street.

The old church was demolished in 1823 when Ferran Street was being built. Its demolition allowed for the Square to be rebuilt as it exists today. Prior to these demolitions, the square was limited to a small angular space, with the rest of the future plaza being occupied by the same church, its cemetery, and the houses of the Magistracy and the General Court of the Veguer.

Jarrod goes over again a bit of the history of the City of Barcelona flag, which has similarities with the English flag of St George because he is patron of Barcelona too, not only England.

In 1137 Ramon Berenguer IV, Count of Barcelona, married Petronila of Aragon, future Queen of Aragon, and then only one year old, with Ramon Rerenguer 23 years her senior. The marriage united all of Catalunya with the Aragon kingdom.

The city of Barcelona was by far the largest settlement in the region. The economy of Barcelona during this period was increasingly directed towards trade. In 1266 James I of Aragon permitted the city to appoint representatives known as consuls to all the major Mediterranean ports of the period. Barcelona was at its high power.

In 1249, James I created the fundamental structure of the municipal government of Barcelona: a board of advisors of 4 members, helped by 8 counselors and an assembly of probi homines (leaders), all of them members of the mà major (Catalan for 'senior hand', or the upper class formed by wealthy merchants).

This Consell de Cent (Council of One Hundred) was the governmental institution of Barcelona established in the 13$^{th}$ century and lasting until the 18$^{th}$ century. After several modifications, by the year 1265, the municipal organization gained its more permanent structure: the municipal authority rested on 3 counselors elected by a Council of one hundred individuals.

The Consell de Cent was abolished by Philip V of Spain with the Decretos de Nueva Planta upon his occupation of Barcelona after the Siege of Barcelona in 1714. Since that moment, the new government of the city was controlled directly by the monarchy.

Jarrod then tells us that a major tradition of Barcelona, the Castellers, often takes place in this square. The origins of this Catalan tradition of building human towers dates back to the 18th century. It was in the small town of Valls, about 40 km west of Barcelona, that the inhabitants started building the towers. The individual groups (colles) started to compete in sporting events. Thus, not only the building of human towers itself was invented, but also the competition.

As we walk off the square, Jarrod points to some Grotesques, or statues of monsters. He makes us notice St George with a dragon underneath him, and a princess on the left. He explains that when water goes through a grotesque statue, they then are called gargoyles. I did not know that.

Jarrod takes us next to The Cathedral of the Holy Cross and Saint Eulalia (Catalan: Catedral de la Santa Creu i Santa Eulàlia), also known as Barcelona Cathedral. This Gothic cathedral is the seat of the Archbishop of Barcelona. The cathedral was constructed from the 13<sup>th</sup> to 15<sup>th</sup> centuries.

It is a pseudobasilica, vaulted over five aisles, the outer two divided into chapels. The transept is truncated. The east end is a chevet of nine radiating chapels connected by an ambulatory. The high altar is raised, allowing a clear view into the crypt. The roof is notable for its gargoyles, featuring a wide range of animals, both domestic and mythical.

We walk inside, where Jarrod points to the wall tiles where the story of a young girl is narrated in Catalan. The cathedral is dedicated to Eulalia of Barcelona, co-patron saint of Barcelona. This young virgin suffered martyrdom in 303, during Roman times. There is a painting of Santa Eulalia while she speaks to soldiers, who offer her a chance to repent her Catholic faith. But she did not repent.

She was subsequently whipped, and then exposed naked in the public square. The legend states that a miraculous snowfall in mid-spring covered her nudity. The choir stalls retain the coats-of-arms of the knights of the Order of the Golden Fleece. The enraged Romans put her then into a barrel with knives stuck into it and rolled it down a street (according to tradition, the one now called Baixada de Santa Eulalia).

She was then crucified on an S shaped cross. The body of Saint Eulalia is entombed in a sarcophagus in the cathedral's crypt. The cathedral has a secluded Gothic cloister where 13 white geese are kept, the number explained by the assertion that Eulalia was 13 years old when she was martyr.

The next stop Jarrod takes us to is the square of San Felipe Neri, in Catalan Plaça of Sant Felip Neri. This square receives its name of the homonymous church of baroque style that presides over it. Gaudí came to pray in this church every day. The square is erected on the old medieval cemetery of Montjuic of the Bishop, destroyed during the Spanish Civil War.

On the walls of the Church of San Felipe Neri, the redoubts of the shrapnel of two bombs launched by the Italian aviation which was helping the rebellious side during the Civil War can still be seen. It was on January 30, 1938 when the first Italian device exploded where the square is now, and then 2.5 seconds later a second bomb exploded.

Most of the forty-two fatalities were children who had gone to take refuge in the church underground. Apart from the deaths, the houses adjacent to the square were also completely destroyed. The municipal architect Adolf Florensa was in charge of the reconstruction project and decided to recreate a square. Every brick was moved here in exactly the same original order.

The square is surrounded by Renaissance-style houses. It is the seat of the old houses of the guilds of Caldereros (coppersmiths) and Zapateros (shoemakers), and Jarrod points to their interesting insignia. In the center of the square is a water fountain with an octagonal base.

Jarrod also lets us know that in the Woody Allen movie Vicky Cristina Barcelona, a scene was filmed in one of the elegant iron balconies overlooking this square. I should watch it again…

We walk then just outside the medieval walls, into Plaça Nova. This 'New Square' of Barcelona opens before the old Porta Praetoria, one of the Roman city gates. From here started the decumanus, one of the main streets where the two aqueducts that carried water to Bàrcino converge.

It was a closed square, typically medieval, until the 1940s, when remodeling following the destruction caused by the civil war bombings opened the Avenue of the Cathedral. Jarrod points to the reproduction of a fragment of the Roman aqueduct. There were originally 76 defense towers along the walls, and we can see now one of the towers at the main entrance, from Plaza Nova into the walls.

Then Jarrod lets us notice a large graffiti mural, by Picasso, reproducing the Easter celebration. There is also a Christmas market in this square in the winter. Speaking of Christmas traditions, Jarrod then goes on to talk about the Caganer.

A Caganer is a figurine depicted in the act of defecation appearing in nativity scenes in Catalunya and neighboring areas. It is most popular and widespread in these areas, but can also be found in other areas of Spain (Murcia), Portugal, and southern Italy (Naples).

The name 'El Caganer' literally means 'the crapper' or 'the shitter.' Traditionally, the figurine is depicted as a peasant, wearing the traditional Catalan red cap (the barretina), with his trousers down, showing a bare backside, and defecating. It appears in Christmas nativity scenes.

There are many possible reasons to have the Caganer, a person in the act of emptying his bowels, in a scene which is widely considered holy. The Caganer, by creating feces, is fertilizing the Earth. It is to signify that what we are taking from nature goes back to nature. This could ensure the nativity scene for the following year, and with it, health of body and peace of mind.

Many modern Caganers represent celebrities and authority figures. By representing them with their pants down, the Caganer serves as a leveling device to bring the mighty down. The Caganer could also represent the spoilsport that we all have inside of us.

It is not surprising that the Caganer was the most beloved figure among the children and, above all, the adolescents, who were already beginning to feel rather like outsiders at the family celebration. Placing this figurine in the nativity scene brings good luck and joy and not doing so brings adversity.

In the Plaça Nova, Jarrod makes us walk closer to the Cathedral's main entrance. It's a beautiful example of Neo-Gothic. Interestingly, it used to be the Headquarters of the Spanish Inquisition.

We then walk on to Sant Pere Santa Caterina i la Ribera, a neighborhood in the Ciutat Vella district of Barcelona. Jarrod points to a Hebrew inscription on the ancient stone blocks on a wall. He says that tombstones were used here to build these buildings.

We keep on walking. It's such a pleasant day. Jarrod stops us on top of a mild incline. He states that we just claimed a mountain. Indeed he points to a plaque on the wall, stating we are 16.9 meters above sea level. It's the highest point in downtown Barcelona, and called Mont Taber. In fact, the street is called Paradise Street, in reference to the fact that this was the closest point to heaven in this city.

Given this was always the highest point, the Temple of August was here in Roman times. It was built around the 1st century BC. We go down a door and some steps, and inside we see that three of the original columns are still preserved.

As we get to the stairs out of where the columns are, Jarrod points to some steps up another direction and a house. This is the Local de Centre Excursionista de Catalunya. Gaudí came to this hiking club.

Plaça del Rei, meaning 'King's Square,' is the next 14th-century medieval public square we visit in the Barri Gòtic of Barcelona. The square is surrounded by the Palau Reial Major including the Saló del Tinell, the Palau del Lloctinent (Lieutenant's Palace), the tower Mirador del Rei Martí (King Martin's Watchtower), and the Capella Reial de Santa Àgata (Royal Chapel of St Agatha).

On its southern side stands Casa Padellàs (Padellàs's House) a 15th–16th century palazzo moved here stone by stone from Mercaders Street in 1931, which since 1943 has housed the Barcelona City History Museum (MUHBA). There are Roman ruins inside.

The tower of King Martin is in honor of an important figure in Barcelona's and Catalunya history. Martin the Humane (29 July 1356 – 31 May 1410), also called the Elder and the Ecclesiastic, was King of Aragon, Valencia, Sardinia and Corsica and Count of Barcelona from 1396 and King of Sicily from 1409 (as Martin II).

Martin was the last of Wilfred the Hairy descendants. Jarrod recounts that Martin was put in a convent with his second wife in an attempt to finally have him conceive an heir. The nouns put a stimulant in his food to help make him fertile and conceive an heir.

He died of the stimulant. He had failed to secure the accession of his illegitimate grandson, Frederic, Count of Luna, and so with him the rule of the House of Barcelona and this Catalan dynasty came to an end.

The marriage of Ferdinand II of Aragon (where Barcelona is) and Isabella I of Castile (where Madrid is) in 1469 united the two royal lines. This is when Spain really became a unified nation, with similar geographic limits as today. Jarrod states that Isabel greeted Christopher Columbus on these steps in this square, Plaça del Rei, as immortalized in paintings.

Madrid became the center of political power while the colonization of the Americas reduced the financial importance (in relative terms) of Mediterranean trade, and so of Barcelona. Catalans could not trade with the newly discovered America. Only Castillans could trade with America.

As we walk past Plaça del Rei, there are few shop windows full of Caganers. One shelf has all politicians, as Trump, Merkel, Obama. Another has all the Barcelona soccer team players. Another an array of other figurines. All have their pants down and are defecating.

Jarrod then states the fact that we are in a 'New Neighborhood,' called el Born. According to legend, the name El Born is derived from the Catalan word 'bornejar' which means to joust. During medieval times jousting tournaments were held on the strip that is now called Passeig del Born.

The location has also been used for religious processions and festivals for hundreds of years. In the 16th century during the Spanish Inquisition, Passeig del Born was the site of the execution of condemned heretics. Some of the streets are named after jobs, as for example 'Silversmith' street. The neighborhood is now one of the most fashionable parts of the city, famous for its international feel, nightlife and wealth of cultural attractions.

In el Born, we walk into the square with an imposing church. Santa Maria del Mar (Saint Mary of the Sea) was built between 1329 and 1383 at the height of Catalunya's maritime and mercantile preeminence. It is an outstanding example of Catalan Gothic, with a purity and unity of style that is very unusual in large medieval building. Jarrod tells us that it was built by working class people from this neighborhood.

We are nearing the end of this great guided tour of Barri Gòtic. Jarrod sits us down a low cement wall, near a modern curved tall red sculpture. El Fossar de les Moreres is a memorial for those killed during the 1713 siege of Barcelona.

The unification of the Spanish kingdoms described above and the riches of the New World were not without political repercussions for Europe. They lead ultimately to the War of the Spanish Succession from 1701 to 1714.

After Charles II died as the last Habsburg king, a battle for Spanish throne ensued between Philip the V vs the Archduke Charles. The Catalan nobility sided with the Habsburgs against the Bourbon Philip V. Barcelona fought valiantly but after 14 months Philip the V entered Barcelona as the winner.

This led to the abolition of Catalan autonomy with the last of the Nueva Planta decrees in 1716, and to the diminution of the political influence of the city of Barcelona in Spain. All Catalan institutions were abolished, the Catalan language was banished. The army stayed to control any rebellion, with the fortress cannons pointing into the city.

The tour is over. We thank and tip Jarrod generously. But the story of Barcelona continues. From the end of the 18th century, the position of Barcelona as a Mediterranean port and the proximity of lignite deposits became important factors in the Industrial Revolution. Catalunya as a whole, and Barcelona in particular, became important industrial centers, with an increase in wealth (if not political power).

In 1812, Barcelona was annexed by Napoleonic France and incorporated into the First French Empire as part of the Montserrat department, where it remained for a few years until Napoleon's defeat.

In 1888, Barcelona hosted the Exposición Universal, which led to a great extension of its urbanized area from Parc de la Ciutadella to Barceloneta. In 1897, the city absorbed six surrounding municipalities and the new district of the Eixample (literally "the extension") was laid out.

During the last week of July 1909, ever since referred to as Tragic Week, the Spanish army clashed with the working classes of Barcelona and other cities of Catalunya. When Prime Minister Antonio Maura mobilized reservists to fight in the Spanish colony of Morocco, the working classes, backed by the anarchists, socialists and republicans, rioted in the streets of Barcelona, resulting in the deaths of over 100 citizens.

The insurrection of the army in July 1936 plunged Spain into civil war. The city, and Catalunya in general, were resolutely Republican. As the power of the Republican government and the Generalitat diminished, much of the city was under the effective control of anarchist groups. The anarchists lost control of the city to their own allies, the Stalinists and official government troops.

Barcelona was repeatedly bombed by air raids. The most severe lasted three days beginning on March 16th, 1938, at the height of the Spanish Civil War. Under the command of the Italian dictator Benito Mussolini, Italian aircraft stationed on Majorca bombed the city 13 times, dropping 44 tons of bombs aimed at civilians.

These attacks were requested by General Franco as retribution against the Catalan population. More than 1,000 people died, including many children, and over 2,000 were injured. The medieval Cathedral of Barcelona was bombed as well, though it did not suffer major damage, and some parts of the Barri Gòtic (the Cathedral neighborhood), including several blocks in front of the cathedral, were damaged. The city finally fell into Nationalist hands on January 26th, 1939.

The resistance of Barcelona to Franco's coup d'état was to have lasting effects after the defeat of the Republican government. The autonomous institutions of Catalunya were abolished and the use of the Catalan language in public life was suppressed and forbidden.

In 1970 the city had a population of over 1.5 million inhabitants. The increase in population led to the development of the metro network, the tarmacking of the city streets, the installation of traffic lights and the construction of the first rondas, or ringroads.

The death of Franco in 1975 brought on a period of democratization throughout Spain. Pressure for change was particularly strong in Barcelona, which considered (with some justification) that it had been punished during nearly forty years of Francoism for its support of the Republican government. Massive, but peaceful, demonstrations on September 11th, 1977 assembled over a million people in the streets of Barcelona to call for the restoration of Catalan autonomy. It was granted less than a month later.

The development of Barcelona was promoted by two events in 1986: Spanish accession to the European Community, and particularly Barcelona's designation as host city of the 1992 Summer Olympics. The process of urban regeneration has been rapid, and accompanied by a greatly increased international reputation of the city as a tourist destination.

Claudia, Daniele and I go get some panini, and take them with us on the metro to reach our next stop. We also get some souvenirs for our loved ones. To switch lines in the metro, we go to an interminable tunnel, apparently hated by Barcelona citizens, which Jarrod had warned us about.

I'm excited we have booked tickets for Park Güell. All the tourist guides say this is a 'must-see' in Barcelona, and Jarrod had remarked a couple of times yesterday on the Gaudí tour that this was worthwhile. Park Güell is a public park composed of gardens and architectonic elements located on Carmel Hill, in Barcelona.

We have quite a few steps to climb to get to the hill and the entrance. The views are beautiful from up here. One can tell there are some interesting structures built on it, but they are mostly hidden in the trees and nature. We wait by a meeting point near the entrance, where we are told the tour will start. But nobody ever shows up.

Once we get better information, we climb some more up the hill to the true meeting point, and meet Joseph, who will be our guide. About 20 others will follow his tour of Park Güell. It's sunny and pleasant. I can't wait. I never get tired when touring interesting places around the world. I'm ready to take lots of notes and pictures.

Joseph starts with some history. From 1800 to 1900 Barcelona went through major changes. Its population increased from 200,000 to 600,000 in those 100 years. In the Gothic quarter where the city was funded the city walls were demolished.

Gaudí met the Güells in the Paris World Fair of 1870. Spain presented leather, in particular leather gloves from Catalunya. Gaudí was commissioned to design the stand. So Gaudí began a relationship with the Güell family who saw his stand in Paris. Gaudí family was very poor, and he was very simple, but Gaudí began to make contacts and changed his life. The new art of Gaudí was seen so far as vulgar, and not appreciated. That would change with time.

What Gaudí and the Güell family had in common is that they were very religious. Joseph our guide in facts points to the many palm trees around us. There is even a holy path to the center of park. Kind of like a Holy Passion.

Around 1899, Güell bought many acres of land on this hill. The site was a rocky hill with little vegetation and few trees, called Muntanya Pelada (Bald Mountain). Güell then employed Gaudí to build an estate for the rich, so that his family – they had eventually 11 kids - could move here, have neighbors and not feel isolated. At that time, the area was considered to be remote from the center of Barcelona.

Gaudí in 1900 was then proposed to divide the land in 69 plots and design grand statues and houses. Eusebi Güell had urbanization in mind. Güell and Gaudí imagined an organized grouping of high-quality homes, decked out with all the latest technological advancements to ensure maximum comfort, finished off with an artistic touch. But after 4 years the Güells stopped the construction. They could only sell 2 plots of land in 4 years. Until 1918 some plots were rented.

The project failed to realize any commercial success. Only two houses were ever built. Then followed an inheritance war, and so Park Güell was eventually sold to the municipality of Barcelona in 1923 and officially opened as a public park in 1926. In 1984, UNESCO declared the park a World Heritage Site under 'Works of Antoni Gaudí.'

The park was built between 1900 and 1914. Park Güell is the reflection of Gaudí's artistic plenitude, which belongs to his naturalist phase (first decade of the 20th century). Gaudí used dynamite to shape the mountain. Architecture and nature for him should be the same. He perfected his personal style through inspiration from organic shapes. He put into practice a series of new structural solutions rooted in the analysis of geometry.

Gaudí added creative liberty and imagination. Starting from a sort of baroquism, his works acquire a structural richness of forms and volumes, free of rational rigidity or any sort of classic premises. In the design of Park Güell, Gaudí unleashed all his architectonic genius and put to practice much of his innovative structural solutions that would become the symbol of his organic style. The multiplicity of symbols found in Park Güell is associated to political and religious signs, with a touch of mystery according to the preferences of that time for enigmas and puzzles.

The park already included a large country house called Larrard House, and was next to a neighborhood of upper class houses called La Salut (The Health). The intention was to exploit the fresh air, well away from smoky factories, and beautiful views from the site. Count Eusebi Güell added to the prestige of the development by moving in 1906 to live in Larrard House. His wife the countess soon began to complain that the gardens were too big.

Ultimately, as I said, only two houses were built, neither designed by Gaudí. One was intended to be a show house, but on being completed in 1904 was put up for sale. As no buyers came forward, Gaudí, at Güell's suggestion, bought it with his savings and moved in with his family and his father in 1906.

This house, where Gaudí lived from 1906 to 1926, was built by Francesc Berenguer in 1904. It contains original works by Gaudí and several of his collaborators. Since 1963 it is the Gaudí House Museum (Casa Museu Gaudí). In 1969 it was declared a historical artistic monument of national interest.

We start walking for the tour by going downhill, and then under a terrace. Joseph describes the fact that there were two roads, going south and going north. Given the low quality of the soil, the trees cannot be very tall. So Gaudí did covered areas to protect people from the sun and from the rain. The countess wanted covered areas, away from carriage roads, so pedestrians could be underneath and carriages above.

The road above our heads, protecting us today from the sun, is held up by tall tree-shaped columns. We are entering the park. This area in the north side was underdeveloped, unfinished. So later architects placed here a garden of seasonal flowers, given the fact that this is a sunny area. Some of the trees here were imported from Austria, and the pines for example are struggling given the poor soil and the heat.

Güell was worth 80 billion dollars in today's money. He had lots of businesses, all over the world. He liked medicine, and cleanliness was an obsession. So everything had to be clean. He wanted a healthy place to live. There are no paintings, and most construction is made of ceramic and cement.

The buildings flanking the entrance, though very original and remarkable with fantastically shaped roofs with unusual pinnacles, fit in well with the use of the park as pleasure gardens and seem relatively inconspicuous in the landscape when one considers the flamboyance of other buildings designed by Gaudí.

Joseph points to Gaudí's ceramic multicolored mosaic salamander, popularly known as 'el drac' (the dragon), at the main entrance, inside a Catalan ship.

There are two entrance buildings. On the left side, the Casa del Guardia. The guardian family still leaves here. Some say it was inspired by a Muslim mosque minaret.

The other building is inspired by the eyes of a fly. There are on top a chimney and a big tower. The predominant blue and white colors were the colors of the Güell family. The cypress pine cone was the inspiration. Once you enlarge the branches, you can make the cross of Jesus. Religious meanings are everywhere.

Joseph then points to a garage-looking structure, where he says the countess' carriage would be parked. The entrance's façade is of Greek inspiration. Gaudí loved Ancient Greece. He thought nothing had been invented after Ancient Greece. The statues at the entrance are mythological.

The icon of the park is this salamander/dragon/serpent or even python that rises prominently on the stairs at the entrance of Park Güell as one of its fountains. It's made of brick and measures 2.4 meters in length. Some say it represents the alchemical salamander, symbolizing fire. Joseph actually says that the 'dragon' in the center in front of us is a crocodile. And that there are two parts of the Nile river on its side.

What's evident is that this animal seems to protect or guard the park. That's why some scholars see the salamander as a representation of the mythological Python at the Oracle of Delphi. In Greek mythology, Python was a great serpent born of mud that was trapped on earth after a great flood. He also guarded the oracle, which was in a cave at Delphi on Mount Parnassus.

When Zeus laid with the goddess Leto, and she was to deliver Artemis and Apollo, Hera was jealous and sent Python (a dragon) to pursue Leto throughout the lands, so that she could not deliver wherever the sun shone. The dragon used to eat people. People prayed to Apollo to kill the dragon.

When Apollo was grown he wanted to avenge his mother's plight and pursued Python, making his way straight for Mount Parnassus where the serpent dwelled, and chased it to the oracle of Gaia at Delphi. There he dared to penetrate the sacred precinct and kill the dragon with his arrows beside the rock cleft where the priestess sat on her tripod. In his honor, ancient Greeks constructed the temple of Apollo.

There are also those who claim that the salamander echoes the crocodile that appears on the coat of arms of the city of Nimes, France, where Güell was raised. Nimes is a city in the south of France. Jeans were invented in Nimes. 'Denim' comes from 'de Nimes', meaning 'from Nimes'. Who ever knew!

Denim was traditionally colored blue with indigo dye to make blue jeans, although 'jean' formerly denoted a different, lighter, cotton fabric. The contemporary use of the word 'jeans' comes from the French word for Genoa, Italy, where the first denim trousers were made.

Güell also studied in Montpellier for two lessons a month. He saw that in Nimes he was always healthy, while he got sick in Montpellier, which was humid with narrow streets. He concluded that the design of Nimes made people healthy. The big park in Nimes must have been what made people healthy, as well as its straight streets.

We walk under what I'll realize later is the terrace. His covered area is the Hall of Columns. Its original name is the Hipóotila Hall, a name that was known in ancient Greece for these great halls with such an arrangement of columns. This one has become a forest of pillars.

There are columns 6.16 meters high and 1.20 meters in diameter around us. Despite there being 86 columns, the initial idea was for there to be 90, but finally Gaudí decided against four of them and in their place put four rosettes of 3 meters in diameter each, representing the 4 seasons of the year, with drawings of 20-tipped suns in different colors.

This area is actually the reservoir of the park. The roof, as will see later, is covered with sand of the beach of Barcelona which is the floor of the terrace above. The water goes through the sand getting purified, then though the columns, and collects below the pavement.

Lots of water was needed at Park Güell, not only for the planned new population, but especially to irrigate the extensive gardens. The drainage system runs through the roof of the park, which was represented by an octopus on the roof.

This room was thought to also become the place where a marketplace would have been. Gaudí designed a market for people to sell fresh products. He wanted to keep it clean, as Count Güell would have wanted. But the problem was that this place had little light.

Lights were eventually placed on top of the columns. There are 16 faces of the moon, for which Gaudí used broken glass, broken plates, and even (for one) shells from the sea. There were also heads of lions on the ceiling, which is the roof of the reservoir, on top of which is the terrace. Joseph as reveals to us that the columns are bent on the perimeter to stop the movement of the building. Wow.

We go up to the large, famous terrace. This is where you usually see photos taken from Park Güell. Not only is it an iconic place in Barcelona, but the views of the city are perfect. It's a 110-metre long snake-shaped balcony that's also an ergonomic bench, designed to perfectly fit the human body.

We are now walking on the sand which Joseph told us was used to filter rain water and feed the reservoir below. This large area was used also to have parties, to let the kids play, for events, even concerts. The reinforced walls are shaped as pantries. On the left Joseph lets us notice a villa built by an original owner.

The benches are the most important feature here on this terrace. They were ordered by the countess Isabel. They were built so rain can go through them. The benches are like a long ergonomic chair, comfortable like an armchair despite being made of hard ceramic and recycled elements. It's said that Gaudí asked workers to sit down here and in this way the bench was made to fit the body of a person. I sit down, relax, and enjoy Gaudí's magic against my tired back.

The curves - like waves - of the serpent bench form a number of enclaves, creating a more social atmosphere. Gaudí incorporated many motifs of Catalan nationalism, and elements from religious mysticism and ancient poetry, into the Park. Much of the design of the benches was the work not of Gaudí but of his often overlooked collaborator Josep Maria Jujol.

Here under Gaudí's project management, Jujol plays with curved forms and Trecandís (Catalan mosaics). The colors and shapes of these small pieces of pottery are scattered all over the bank randomly and, at times, with some sense too. If you look closely, you'll find signs of the zodiac, stars, fish, flowers and religious motifs. Green, blue and yellow predominate, which for Gaudí represented hope, faith and charity.

On the outside of the balcony you'll find the gargoyles in the form of lion heads that are part of the water drainage system. This area is also known as Plaça de la Natura. Unlike the rest of the park's constructions that mimic nature by forming part of it, this space is built partly on the mountain and partly on the Hipóstila Room that supports it.

This area, then called the Greek Theatre, was intended precisely for that, to be a theatre. And the idea was that the owners of the houses around the estate could see the shows directly from their terraces.

Joseph lastly makes us notice Gaudí' house, and the top of the mountain with the cross of Jesus. He concludes that the plan for Park Güell did not succeed because it was just too far away from Barcelona's center, and there was no public transportation. This presented a problem especially for the boss of each family, i.e. the lady of the house, who would feel a bit stranded and isolated here.

What an interesting place this Park Güell was. I'm sure there are a thousand other secrets about it to discover. But more fun awaits me, as I'm supposed to meet with my high school friend Paolo later in the afternoon. With Claudia and Daniele, trusted and wonderful trip companions, we head down a few hundred stairs from the hill back towards the metro.

Claudia saves me as she has a recharger with which I can give life back to my iPhone, which had gone dead. I did not even have access to Paolo's address anymore! Thank you Claudia! I can now message Paolo, who gives me detailed direction on what metros to take, and exactly how to get to his place.

The metro takes me a couple of blocks from Paolo's apartment, on Carrer del Parliament. I find his building fairly easily, and take the lift to his floor. He leaves in a very nice apartment, in a central area in Barcelona, and has bought the apartment just a few years ago.

I've been friend with Paolo since our first year of high school, in 1978, when we were 14 years old. He is a wonderful person, kind and gentle, very smart. I think we were desk mates one year in school together. He was always very friendly with all the girls. Outgoing, witty, at times funny in his being critical of so many things wrong in Italy back then, like politics, bigot religious culture, etc.

He has always been super nice and hospitable. He offers me all kinds of food and drink, and I gladly accept coffee – unusual for me, but I'm fairly tired, and still have a lot ahead of me, and plenty of water. I ask him about the apartment, which I'm impressed with, and he says he paid 270,000 euros for it. Paolo is a pneumologist (lung specialist) who also is an anesthesiologist, and he now works in a private eye hospital. He likes his job, which is not too stressful and pays relatively well.

We soon talk via computer to his lovely mother, who I was always fond of. She is so sweet, like Paolo, and her voice has not changed in these 39 years. She has always been so close to Paolo, and they have had a loving relationship, which I can tell continues now.

Back when I was leaving in Manhattan, in the early 1990's, Paolo had called me from Italy. He said he was coming to NY in a couple of months, and I enthusiastically offered him to stay in my one bedroom apartment in the lower east side, near the Brooklyn Bridge.

His professional career had been interesting and eventful. He graduated from medical school from our local University of Chieti, then done a Pulmonary (lung) residency in Naples, where he stayed and worked for a few years. He then had moved to Milan, and eventually had done another residency, this time in anesthesia.

But a couple of weeks after the original phone call, Paolo called me again. I was not expecting this second phone call. He said, "Vincenzo, I need to tell why I'm coming to New York." "Sure Paolo, go ahead." "I'm coming to compete in the Gay Games. I'll be swimming in the Gay Games, which are in New York this year."

One of the things I most appreciate in life is the chance to share one's innermost feelings and secrets to each other. I was really moved by Paolo's confession. Going back to our childhood in Pescara, Italy, I do not recall one friend who had admitted to being gay. Not one.

Thinking back, I should have known, and maybe I did, that Paolo was gay. He never went out with a girl, but was always with them; he was their confidant. He seemed more at ease with them than some of the more macho guys, who he detested. He was also so gentle, kind, caring.

He later confided that he moved from Naples, a city he adores, because he would be beaten up there as gay. He eventually left Milan in search of meritocracy, the sun, and more tolerance. He found it all here in Barcelona.

Later we leave his apartment, and go for a long walk around Barcelona, eventually ending up on the coast, in Barceloneta.

Paolo is an intellectual in a sense, knows everything, and he is a wonderful guide around Barcelona.

He later says, "Barcelona lo tiene todo," meaning Barcelona has got everything. In fact I know now Barcelona has history, culture, opportunities, wonderful people, great weather, the beach... everything I love. And Paolo found here even more than that.

He confides in me that he has a new boyfriend. His love stories, and I've heard of a few over the years, have never been easy. He is very excited about this one. His boy is from Barcelona, about his age, formerly married and with a teenage daughter. This one sounds like a wonderful guy.

I'm so blessed to have a friend like Pablito. He is the quintessential friend. Loyal, someone who I highly admire, and someone who is always there for his friend, 100%, even if we just talk about once a year, and see each other probably every five. Everytime, it's like if we saw each other yesterday. He confides his inner feelings to me, I do the same with him, trusting his good advice, and his altruism. He knows where I come from, my beliefs, my true self.

I manage to help organize (Paolo makes the reservations) dinner all together, with Paolo, Juan Antonio (his boyfriend), Daniele, Maurizia (Daniele's sister), Simone (Daniele's sister's boyfriend), and Claudia. Paolo and Juan Antonio hold hands. They seem in love, what a wonderful site. Paolo highly deserves it.

We have a lot of specialties I enjoy, such as small bites of boiled and lightly fried potatoes with a wonderful mayonnaise-like sauce called Las patatas bravas, a potato frittata called Tortilla de patate, a wonderful cured pork cut very very thin called El jamon asado – perhaps my most favorite among all of them being favorites!, uncooked fresh baccala' with thinly sliced onions and tomatoes called La esqueixada de bacalao, slices of excellent bread with tomatoes brushed on top similar to the Italian 'bruschetta' called Pan con tomate.

The Catalan beer I have is called Voll Damm, very good. We have also several desserts. I order a flan with lots of whipped cream, others have a Catalan almond cakes called Torta de Santiago, as well as chocolate cake and other delicious treats. We finish at 12:30am, after talking in several languages – Catalan and Italian in particular, but also English, about everything, from love to politics to family to our works to our countries. It's so true that the number one key to happiness is social relations.

**Sunday March 12th, 2017**

This is the day of departure back to the USA. I've had a great time here in Barcelona. Got done all I wanted to. Interacted with wonderful friends and colleagues. As usual, both the academic part and the social parts were superb.

At breakfast in our hotel, I see and salute Moshe, thanking him for the invitation. He is supernice, as usual, and already puts further plans in my calendar, such a future congress in Florence in 2019. We have lots of plans together.

Back in my room, I pack. The cleaning people have folded even my dirty laundry. What service. It's really sad I have to leave such a wonderful place. I take a quick and easy taxi ride to the airport.

Barcelona has a huge airport, really international, planes are leaving from here to all continents. You feel at the center of everything. We are indeed not far from the middle of Europe, almost attached to Africa, a short hop to America, and Asia is not far. It's still amazing to me, as usual, how many people there are at airports and around the world.

While waiting, I speak with my wonderful parents. What a happy couple they are, always so happy to see me happy. They seem perfectly ok to stay home and relax: will I ever become like them?? I just cannot picture it now, but I do know we do change some overtime. Some day…

I talk also with my sister Anna; the more time goes by, the more I love her. She is a pillar in my life. She understands me well, and knows my strengths and weaknesses, probably better than even me. I trust her judgment enormously. I look up to her. Nobody is perfect, but she has been a soulmate for me on this beautiful journey which is life.

The plane from Barcelona to London is delayed. I begin to get a bit worried I won't be able to catch the connection for the London to Philadelphia flight. But there is not much I can do about it. I've learned not to stress about these issues anymore, if I cannot control them anyway. We finally take off from gorgeous Barcelona.

About 20 minutes before landing, the stewardess comes to my row, row 7, and says, looking at me, "Philadelphia?" I'm dreading what comes next. Other people across the isle going to Boston I think have been rebooked, she has said they were going to stay in a hotel in London overnight, and leave the next day.

I really do not want to do that. Tomorrow I'm supposed to work, in fact to start at 7am since I'm on service in the hospital. I would really like not to dump all my work on my trusted colleagues. But the lady goes on, "You have been rebooked. You will leave London tomorrow. Just go to a BA (British Airways) desk when you land, and they will tell you the details of the rebooking, and give you the reservation for the hotel overnight."

I beg, "But can't I try make it?" She goes, "You'll never make it. Sorry." I'm not happy, but I guess I'm stuck. Sometimes in life you just have to accept your destiny, and carry on. I begin to think about this fate, and making the most of it. My beloved nephew Vincenzo, my sister's son, lives in London. As soon as I land, I think, I'll send him a WhatsApp. He'll be delighted we can spend the evening and night together.

While we begin our descent to London, I can tell a couple of young girls are planning something. I bet they also have a close connection, and want to try to make it. About 10 minutes before landing, the loud speaker states sternly, "For those of you who have been rebooked for tomorrow's flight, please stay in Terminal 3 (the terminal where we are about to land). Do not go to other terminals, as the BA staff in terminal 3 is the one who will rebook you and give you the hotel voucher."

Uhm... I think, they must be aware some – maybe these kids – want to try to make their connections anyway, and are doing all they can to avoid them from trying to.

What am I going to do? I know Heathrow well. It's huge. I know I even have to switch terminals, as the flight I'm no longer booked at leaves from Terminal 5. I do agree with the stewardess, it would be next to impossible to get through miles of corridors and a few escalators, and then security at terminal 3, then get the shuttle to Terminal 5, which I know takes a while, then again go through miles of corridors, passport control, a few more escalators up and down, then through international security for baggage - where there is always a line, then towards the gate, I'm not even sure which one, probably quite a hike after the baggage check.

But if you reader know me a bit, you have already guessed what I'm going to try to do anyway. I never give up.

We land at 4:10pm. The jetway takes its time, so I'm out of the plane at 4:20pm. My ticket for Philadelphia, printed this morning at the hotel and now seemingly already old and crumpled, says that I have to get through security (where, I wonder? which one?) by 4:35pm. That they'll close the plane by 4:55pm.

As soon as I'm out of the plane, I start running. My carryon bag and professional bag on top are quite heavy, plus I'm dragging on top of them my red sweater and my coat. The hallways as predicted are seemingly endless, like you can see the horizon at the end of them.

I have to climb a few escalators, which I do carrying all my luggage, seemingly 50 pounds worth. Quite an effort, despite the fact that I'm a big guy. Often I hesitate for a second on taking the lift (elevator) or the escalators, and I sometimes make the right decision, sometimes not.

After what seems like an eternity - but it's probably only 6-7 minutes - I get to a glass gate for the bus to terminal 5. The two girls from my plane who had planned to make their connection against what the stewardess had advised them, and a mother with son, are waiting behind the gate.

I ask the girls where they are going. They said they are going to Boston, their plane is supposed to leave at 4:40pm, but boarding started a few minutes late, so they are hoping. They were also told they were rebooked for tomorrow, and told to get the voucher for the hotel and all the information at Terminal 3 in the BA help desk.

I'm happy I'm not alone in being crazy. They have not done any of that, and we all would have to go back if we, as it's almost certain, do not make our planes.

A minute after I've arrived to this point, another young girl from our plane arrives. I ask her where she is going. She says she is on my same flight, the 5:10pm (17:10) going to Philadelphia. She says we have 9 minutes to clear security at Terminal 5. As there is no sign of a bus or something (something!) to take us to terminal 5, we are both pessimistic.

But about 3 minutes later a man does open the glass doors, and shows us to the bus to Terminal 5. We hop on.

Four hurried passengers. Three have to make their college classes - the Boston girls at Boston College, the Philadelphia girl (from Paris apparently) has to make her University of Pennsylvania classes. They are all juniors. One of the Boston girls gets texted that their friends on their flight have boarded, could not wait for them anymore. They guess they'll never make it.

So, when a couple of minutes later (but it feels a lot longer than that) we arrive at Terminal 5, the Boston girls let the Penn student and me step off first as we might have a better chance of making our plane.

The French girl takes off in a sprint, she has almost nothing with herself to carry. I pretend I can keep up with my 50 pounds of wobbly, disorganized bags and clothing. Escalator one, Corridor one. A couple of more escalators. Another interminable corridor.

Then I take the lift - good choice, the elevator car is right there (!), and on the next level I see at the end of the corridor signs for Terminal 5 passport control. The Penn student is actually catching up to me as we enter the queue, she must have taken the wrong turn just earlier in this corridor, I'm glad I guessed right.

I let her step in front of me. The line is probably about 50 people long anyway. I doubt we would ever make it through it in less than 5 minutes, which is the time when apparently they will not let us through, at 4:35pm (16:35).

The Penn girl pulls a wonderful move though at this point, she start going under the barriers, avoiding the whole line!! I'm afraid she'll get arrested, or at least get yelled at by the 50 already in line. I'm sure we are not the only ones with close (well, our is impossible) connections.

But no one moves. As she is under about the third of the 7 or 8 bands to go through to get to the front of the line and passport control, I start following her. What the hell! Nobody is yelling. The security staff is a tall thin man with a big smile, and he lets us be her first and me second in line. The security officer in the booth right in front of us is a nice middle-aged British lady. The Penn girl goes through her in a flash!! We are in business, I think.

I move right to her booth. By now I'm sweating pretty good. She smiles gently. She checks my ticket, my passport, gives them back to me, saying, "You made it, now you have time, you do not have to rush anymore."

She knows it's like she is giving me a huge gift. So I gather again my luggage, and start sprinting (I know, I do not need to, but... I guess I sprint through life normally, while not continue now?), but at my second step I hear "Hold on Sir!"

Who said it? To whom? I turn around, and the nice security lady says to come back, "Your booking has been canceled, you are no longer on this flight." I look at her computer panel, and a red 'x' takes about a quarter of it. Unmistakable. "Oh no!!!!!!" I think inside. I do not know what to say. How come the Penn girl before me got through? I guess after all I won't make it. And I am here!! (almost...)

The lady goes, "Where you with the girl before you?" I lie, softspoken, "Yes." She picks up the phone, and dials a couple of quick numbers. I mutter, "Can I be put back in the plane please?", but I doubt she hears it. But she can read it in my sweat that she'd make me really happy if I can make the plane.

She is on the phone for a couple of minutes, talking to different people. She says I'm traveling with the lady who just got through. Then silence. Now all 50 poor travelers I jumped in front of are not so ok anymore with having been so kind to let me through. The line is stuck. The other security officers also are not clearing the other travelers, so everyone is waiting. Will I be lynched?

When I'm beginning to think how to make it back to Terminal 3, get the hotel information, and boarding passes for tomorrow flight, and call my nephew Vincenzo, and inform my family in Philadelphia, I see the red 'x' disappear from the security lady's computer, and a green check mark appear. She hands me the paper ticket I had given her, and says with a big smile, "You are all good sir." I could marry her!!

I'm still unsure if they'll really want me on the plane. Where am I booked? Had they sold my seat? Are there any more seats? Will I have to 'bargain' with more BA officers? At the gate? Where? Will they have any record of me? Will they be mad I did not follow instructions, directions? That I got through passport security perhaps only because a lady took pity on me, hoping the next officers would too?

A few more corridors. A few more escalators. A lift. Then baggage control. Of course, I still have to go through baggage control. There are probably 15 people in the line I pick. I do not have the stomach to ask them to jump in front of them. The UPenn girl is long gone, she must have made it. At least I hope so. Will she put a good word for me? She does not even know me, or my name.

After another two to three minutes, I get to put my luggage on the rolling belt. I take all my staff off, all my pockets are full, passports, pendrive, penn, handkerchief, wallet, iPhone, a few coins of euros and fractions of euros, I have to take off my belt, put red sweater, black coat, overstaffed blue professional bag and almost overflowing red carryon on the belt.

As the blue bag is just out of my reach, I tell the officer, "There is water in there!" He is nice enough to catch it before it enters the tunnel, hands it to me, and I find the bottle right away.

As he asks me "To do want to dump it or drink it?" I'm already googling it down.

I pass the security gate myself no problem, I got nothing on me. But then I bump in another big issue. On the other side of the tunnel security machine, I notice my blue bag has not made it to this side, but was diverted across the glass to the parallel downward ramp.

I realize, as others are and point out to me, that going to that side are bags that need further hand checking! No!!!! I do not have my iPhone on me, but by now we must be close if not after 16:55, or 4:55pm, so the time that the gate closes. And I still do not even know the number of the gate, or the gate area. Behind me, I see that there are areas 'A,' 'B,' 'C,' 'D,' and 'E' at least. Great! (sarcastic)

To my despair, the lady who is checking the bags on the monitors looks at me as my large red carryon is going through. "Is this you bag sir?" It might sound nasty while you are reading her phrase, but she actually says it nicely. She is just doing her job.

She says, "Do you have jam in there sir?" Dammed it!! "Yes I do, two small jars," I mimic their size, less that 100cc, I know it's legal. I do not know what else to say. Then, stupidly, "You can keep them if you want." But with a friendly smile. Soon after, I see this red bag of mine follow the same further belt as my bleu bag. It's getting checked too.

I gather my passports, handkerchief, coins, pendrive, tickets, wallet, iPhone (I never look at the time through this all endeavor, no point to do so), belt. Then I wait. Everyone can see I'm sweating like a madman. But I'm not making a scene. No point. There are also four or five other bags to check before my two ones. This will take forever I think. I switch back thinking how I'll undo all this and get back to Terminal 3 and tomorrow's flight. Oh my!

Finally (may be a minute or two later, but to me another eternity) a couple of officers start going through the bags on the others side and check them. There are at least five passengers ahead of me waiting for these bags.

Eventually the officers point to the blue bag, and I raise my hand. The bigger of the two officers lifts it, and takes it to another table a few yards away, as the main area is already overcrowded. He seems ok, not super-friendly but probably not mean. My life - it feels to me – is in his hands.

He discovers a bunch of small toothpastes (tiny), contact lenses container, and places then out of my beauty case and into a plastic bag. He looks in every nook and cranny in the large bag – and there are at least four difference large and deep sections, three zippers, etc.

"Hold on to your bag," he says when done. "I'll have to check this through the machine again," he says grabbing the few personal hygiene items he had just identified. It takes forever for the machine to check these tiny items.

In the meanwhile, I spot back in my original location at the end of the security check where my bags went through that my red carryon is next to be checked. I move swiftly towards there, but the officer warns me not to move, that I should come only when my first bag is cleared. "Great again," I think, sarcastically.

My blue bag gets cleared; I put all the tiny items very disorganizedly back in, and move to where my red carryon is. This is where the two small jam containers are, so we know the culprit here. I help the friendly security officer locate them; I remember exactly where they are. They have to run these too through the machine.

The friendly security officer, seeing me still sweat like I just showered, takes pity on me. I ask, "What is the fastest way to get to the gates?" as I see another labyrinth of options in front of us. "Do you know your gate sir?" "I do not," I answer, a bit defeated. "Well, while we ran the machine, go over there to those panels, it will tell you."

I run over, only about 50 yards. In my head, "Let's see… 17:10 (5:10pm) - they are listed by departure time, … Philadelphia,… here it is… gate B34." And then next to it, in bold black letters, "FIRST CLOSING." Argh!!!

I get back to the security check and my now friends, the two security officers. "B34", I mutter, "but it also says 'First closing.'" "It's going to be that way," one of them points to the right long corridor, where I can only see 'All gates' written. "You might make it if you run real fast. Escalators are down there." Great, of course, more escalators, thank you.

In the meanwhile, they have not given me back my red carryon. I look in the machine inside where they had put it. The screen at that exact moment lights up. "ALARM" is the large red neon sign now on it.

Both officers go near the machine now. "What now," I think? I do not know what could be wrong. Did someone who recently did cocaine touched my bag at some point? When?

The screen had said 'First closing.' The officer had said "You MIGHT make it if you run real fast." This further delay will be the last drop, the one causing me to miss this plane. Well...

Miraculously, the officer clears the bag with not much more time. I'm so discombobulated by now I'm not sure how they do it. May be they just override the machine, or ignore the warning. Being as it may, the bag is back finally to me less than a minute after the alarm sign went on. I reconstruct the pyramid of clothes and bags, and I take off on the right.

Was it gate B34? I do not want to stop and recheck. I head for the escalator down, but right in front of me about 15 people, slow moving, are approaching it. I divert around them to the second option, the lifts I had bypassed. Excellent choice. As soon as I hit the bottom, one of the doors to the lifts opens. I dart in. Just one floor down.

Then I begin to follow signs. Corridor to B gates. Then another to B32-56. Then I turn towards 'B32-35'. I must be getting close. Now I'm really sprinting. I do not want to lose one more second. This is all up to me now, and I want to have no regrets.

I actually try to make a bit of noise as I run as I see over 100 yards away first Gate B35, then B34, then B 33, then B32. By now

I'm not so sure of what the exact number is. I doubt much blood is getting to my brain.

As I sprint by B35 and I'm approaching B34 zipping by it, a nice officer goes, "Philadelphia?" "Yes!" I reply elated. It's not B32. It's B34!! They found me!!

It's amazing I make the plane. I'm the last one on. I'm sweating like a pig. My shirt is drenched. A few more seconds and I would not have made it. The check-in person says: "Good run. You must be Berghella. We were just going to close the plane." I love traveling ☺.

# Acknoledgements

Paola Luzi

www.ingramcontent.com/pod-product-compliance
Lightning Source LLC
LaVergne TN
LVHW011337080426
835513LV00006B/408